PRINTMAKING IN NEW MEXICO
1880–1990

Gustave Baumann (1881–1971), *San Geronimo—Taos*, ca. 1918–22,
color woodcut, image 178 x 152 mm (7 x 6 in), printed by the artist.
Collection, Museum of Fine Arts, Museum of New Mexico, Santa Fe,
acquired with funds from the School of American Research [886]

PRINTMAKING
IN NEW MEXICO
1880–1990

Clinton Adams

UNIVERSITY OF NEW MEXICO PRESS

Albuquerque

Library of Congress Cataloging in Publication Data

Adams, Clinton, 1918–
Printmaking in New Mexico, 1880–1990 / Clinton Adams.
p.   cm.
Includes bibliographical references.
ISBN 0-8263-1307-8
ISBN 0-8263-1259-4 (pbk.)
1. Prints, American—New Mexico.   2. Prints—19th century—New Mexico.
3. Prints—20th century—New Mexico.   I. Title.
NE535.N6A33   1991
769.9789—dc20
90-47752
CIP

Photo Credits

References are to illustration and plate numbers. Plates I through VIII follow page 70; Plates IX through XVI follow page 102. Except as noted below, all photographs are by Damian Andrus, Albuquerque.

Albuquerque Museum: 43; Boston Public Library (Stein and Mason): 10, 11; Jerry Bywaters Collection on Art of the Southwest, Hamon Arts Library, Southern Methodist University: 37; Museum of Fine Arts, Santa Fe (Blair Clark): 6, 7, 9, 12, 15–19, 23, 25, 31, 32, 39–42, 45, 46, 50, 54, 57, 61, 67, 95, Frontispiece, II, IV–VII, IX, XI; Roswell Museum and Art Center: 1, 2, 53; Spencer Museum of Art, University of Kansas: 26; Syracuse University Art Collections: 33; Tamarind Institute: 65, 66, 69, 73, 78; University Art Museum, University of New Mexico: 27.

Garo Antreasian: 81, XIII; Robert Arber: 91, XI; Stephen Britko, Naravisa Press: 96; Richard L. Fallin: 94; Spencer Fidler: 85; Hand Graphics, Ltd.: 92, 93; Harper House, Dallas: VIII; Jason Jones: 74, 77; Jim Kraft, Unified Arts: 97, 98, XII; Robert Reck: 49, 79, 83, 85, 99, 100; Anthony Richardson: XV; Seymour Tubis: 86, 87; Donald David Woodman: 70.

CONTENTS

Preface   •   *vii*

CHAPTER 1
The Early Years   •   *1*

CHAPTER 2
Before and During
the Great Depression   •   *15*

CHAPTER 3
After the War   •   *25*

CHAPTER 4
Tamarind:
Los Angeles to Albuquerque   •   *40*

CHAPTER 5
The Contemporary Scene   •   *57*

Notes   •   *141*

Bibliography   •   *151*

Index   •   *159*

PREFACE

T HIS BOOK HAD ITS BEGINNING in an invitation to write a short essay on the history of printmaking in New Mexico for inclusion in *The Art of New Mexico*, a book in preparation by the Museum of Fine Arts in Santa Fe. As I began my study, I found—not to my surprise—that the subject was much too large to be confined within the space of that essay, portions of which have been incorporated (in different form) within the present text.

I have defined printmaking in New Mexico to include prints made by artists who have lived here, and prints made by visitors who have been affected in some degree by what they saw or experienced here. I have excluded monotypes and photographs, not because of a lack of regard for either medium, but in order to give emphasis to the traditional media of the printmaker. It will be evident that I have not sought to maintain a balanced objectivity, that I have instead given disproportionate emphasis to the work of some artists whom I consider to be of particular significance.

My principal criterion has been the intent of the artist as expressed in his or her work. From Rembrandt to Picasso, the world's finest prints have been made by artists who use a graphic process *graphically*. The fact that the process makes possible multiple impressions from the plate, stone, or block often has been of less interest to these artists than its intrinsic qualities as a creative medium. Not all artists use the print in this way. For some, particularly those with social concerns, the multiplicity of the print is important as a means for dissemination of ideas. For others, multiplicity has provided a commercial incentive. Economic motives were not uncommon among the early painters of New Mexico; that they remain a force today is made evident by the "decorator prints" that flourish in the galleries of Taos and Santa Fe. I have purposely avoided inclusion of such work among the illustrations.

It is my hope that what I have written may cause others to recognize that a number of fine prints have been made in New Mexico and that they are worthy of further study. Students seeking topics for theses and dissertations will find a wealth of them: artists about whom little has been written, and large bodies of work that have not been catalogued. When such research is undertaken, it will doubtless reveal errors and omissions in what I have written.

I express my appreciation to David Turner, director of the Museum of Fine Arts, for his encouragement to pursue this topic—both in this book and as guest curator of a special exhibition. Many members of the museum's staff have assisted in my research, foremost among them curator Sandra D'Emilio, who has assisted my research in important ways; Susan Benforado, formerly curator of contemporary art, who made helpful comments on an early version of my text; and registrar Diane Block, who gave me critical aid in assembly of illustrations. All those who study the history of art in New Mexico are indebted to the curators and librarians who have compiled and maintained the museum's indispensable clipping files, particularly Edna C. Robertson and Phyllis Cohen.

I am likewise indebted to the staff of the University Art Museum, University of New Mexico. Director Peter Walch, associate director Linda Bahm, curator Diana Gaston, and curatorial assistants Kira Sowanick and Melissa Strickland have been particularly helpful. Joseph Traugott, Tiska Blankenship, and MaLin Wilson assisted me in use of the research archives at the Jonson Gallery.

My friend Earl Stroh provided many insights from his long experience in Taos; David L. Witt, curator at the Harwood Foundation, provided information; and Elmer Schooley generously shared knowledge and memories. David Farmer read a preliminary version of the manuscript and contributed essential information about the work of artists who came to New Mexico from Oklahoma and Texas. Frederick Black gave me the benefit of his experience at the Museum of Fine Arts; he and Dorothy Skousen Black made several suggestions which have enabled me to write a more balanced account of the events of the 1950s. Van Deren Coke brought to my attention works that I might otherwise have overlooked, and Arnold E. Ronnebeck provided information about his father's work.

In their lifetimes it was my privilege to converse at length with Kenneth M. Adams, Howard Cook, Andrew Dasburg, Randall Davey, Raymond Jonson,

Barbara Latham, Ward Lockwood, Frederick O'Hara, Georgia O'Keeffe, John Sommers, Mitchell A. Wilder, and Adja Yunkers; I wish I had thought to ask them questions that now come to mind. The late Kerstin Lucid shared her memories of the years that she and Adja Yunkers lived in Albuquerque.

Other artists, printers, curators, and scholars to whom I am indebted for assistance include David Acton, Garo Antreasian, Robert Arber, Robert Blanchard, Judy Booth, Robert Brady, Stephen Britko, Joan Clark, Robert Conway, Michael Costello, Marjorie Devon, Teresa Hayes Ebie, Peter Eller, Connie Fox, Bethany Fuller, Lez Haas, Russell Hamilton, Sinclair H. Hitchings, Domenic J. Iacono, Gene Kloss, Jim Kraft, John Palmer Leeper, William Lumpkins, Alexander Masley, Ila McAfee, Dorothy McCray, Frank McCulloch, James C. Moore, Jane Myers, Tom Palmore, Jeffrey Ryan, Wesley A. Rusnell, Rebecca Schnelker, Michele Bourque Sewards, Vera Henderson Sprunt, Seymour Tubis, Linda Tyler, Robert Walters, Harry Westlund, Robert R. White, and Virginia Yen. Above all others, I thank the artists who have generously granted permission for reproduction of their work, and the museums which have provided photographs of works in their collections. These are individually acknowledged in captions to the illustrations.

To Elizabeth C. Hadas, director of the University of New Mexico Press, and her able staff, I extend appreciation for the friendly and efficient way in which this book has been advanced to publication. Dana Asbury, who has served as its editor, is a master of her craft; her helpful suggestions and genuine interest have made work with her a pleasure. Milenda Nan Ok Lee has brought together the words and pictures in a clean and straightforward design.

My wife Mary has been patiently supportive throughout the strains and pressures that accompany the writing of any book, large or small; for her understanding, as always, I express my love and appreciation.

Clinton Adams
Albuquerque, 1990

PRINTMAKING IN NEW MEXICO
1880–1990

CHAPTER 1

THE EARLY YEARS

F EW OF THE PAINTERS who came to New Mexico in the early years of the twentieth century, when art colonies were first established in Taos and Santa Fe, thought of printmaking as a creative activity. For most American artists, "printing and painting were separate and unequal endeavors. Graphic arts were a practical means for the artistically inclined to earn a living, but were not considered either an artist's medium or profession."[1] The European tradition of the *peintre-graveur*—the painter who also makes prints—was far distant from American practice; here, most prints were reproductive in nature, engraved or drawn by anonymous craftsmen after the designs of artists, and for this reason, neither received nor merited the serious attention accorded to painting and sculpture.

The low esteem in which American prints were for so long held accounts for the fact that so few critics or historians wrote seriously about them. This was particularly true in New Mexico, where, despite all that has been written about the artists of Taos and Santa Fe, their work as printmakers has been neglected, with consequent gaps in our knowledge.[2] There are, unfortunately, many things we do not know about the beginnings of printmaking in New Mexico; much of the record has disappeared.

The early Taos artists—Oscar Berninghaus, Ernest L. Blumenschein, E. Irving Couse, Herbert (Buck) Dunton, Bert Phillips, Joseph Sharp, and Walter Ufer—shared the common view of printmaking. Lithography, in particular, was unhappily identified in their minds with nineteenth-century chromolithographs which, produced in the millions by an established industry, had

1 Peter Moran (1841–1914), *A Burro Train, New Mexico*, 1880 [Keppel 30], etching, image 175 x 245 mm (6⅞ x 9⅝ in), printed by Kimmel and Voight, New York. Collection, Roswell Museum and Art Center, purchase, Patricia Gaylord Anderson Memorial Fund [79.48]

"flooded the country with poor designs, wretchedly carried out,"[3] and, in the process, had served to establish the word *chromo* as a synonym for the common and vulgar. The fact that many artists, Berninghaus and Ufer among them, had served as lithographers' apprentices before becoming professional painters may have further conditioned their attitude.

Although etching enjoyed a better reputation than lithography, most of the artists who participated in the etching revival of the 1880s and 1890s were specialist-printmakers—artists who only made prints—and many of these were women, thought to be "dilettantes who made art for pleasure only."[4] The etchers of the late nineteenth century nonetheless contributed importantly to an increased interest in printmaking among American painters. The etchings of James McNeill Whistler were widely collected and admired, as were those

2

2 Peter Moran (1841–1914), *Harvest at San Juan*, 1882–83 [Keppel 74], etching, image 155 x 312 mm (6¹/₈ x 12¹/₄ in), printed by Kimmel and Voight, New York. Collection, Roswell Museum and Art Center, purchase, Patricia Gaylord Anderson Memorial Fund [79.47]

of Seymour Haden, Thomas Moran, and Frank Duveneck, with whom Sharp and Ufer had studied in Cincinnati.[5] Peter Moran (Thomas Moran's younger brother) appears to have been the first artist to make etchings of New Mexican subjects. His prints ranged from the direct observation of *A Burro Train, New Mexico* to the more romantic *Harvest at San Juan*, in which the dramatic contrasts of dark and light reflect the sophisticated conventions of European landscape painting.

1

2

Despite these precedents, it was not until 1913, ten years after Whistler's death, that, perhaps stimulated by inclusion of a large number of important European prints in the Armory Show of 1913, an increasing number of American painters began to make prints. In 1917 their activity culminated in the founding of the Painter-Gravers of America, an organization that included

3

among its members many of the leading painters of the time, and that had as its purpose to ensure recognition of the fine print as a legitimate medium for creative expression.[6]

Even so, painting was paramount during the years in which the Taos and Santa Fe art colonies came to prominence. The newly organized Taos Society of Artists held its first group exhibition in 1915,[7] and within the next few years its members attracted national attention as frequent recipients of prizes and awards in exhibitions at the National Academy of Design and the Art Institute of Chicago. The exotic allure of Taos and Santa Fe "gave New Mexico's art centers an unrivaled status among other American summer colonies"[8] and, supported by the extensive advertising campaigns of the Santa Fe Railway, did much to ensure that a steady stream of artists would make their way to New Mexico before and during World War I.

Few of the early arrivals made prints. Among the founders of the Taos Society of Artists, Dunton was the most prolific, but his lithographs are pedestrian both in imagination and execution. Berninghaus was a good reporter, and in such prints as *Street Scene, Taos*, he provides an accurate, carefully rendered image of Taos at the beginning of the century.

Gerald Cassidy came to Albuquerque in 1890 and to Santa Fe in 1912. Like Sharp and Ufer, Cassidy had studied in Cincinnati with Frank Duveneck, who encouraged him to work as a commercial lithographer and illustrator. Cassidy soon gained recognition in New York as "one of the best commercial lithographers in the profession,"[9] a conclusion well supported by such prints as his elegant *Portrait of Mrs. M.*, drawn in 1916. Cassidy also made lithographs of New Mexico subjects, including his freshly drawn *Sand Storm*, a print that vividly depicts the hardships of travel in the American West.[10]

Ralph M. Pearson, a painter and etcher who had been liberated by the Armory Show from "the straitjackets of convention,"[11] took up residence on a ranch south of Taos in 1915 (the year he received a silver medal in etching at the Panama-Pacific Exposition). Pearson apparently brought his etching press to the ranch either in 1915 or shortly thereafter, for by 1918 he had produced a number of etchings sufficient for an exhibition in Santa Fe.[12] It was in the same period that Birger Sandzen began to visit and work in New Mexico, characteristically drawing and painting directly from the landscape. Sandzen, who became active as a lithographer in 1916, had studied art both in his native Sweden and in Paris with the modernist painter-printmaker Edmond François Aman-Jean before emigrating to Kansas in 1894.

4

3 O. E. Berninghaus (1874–1952), *Street Scene, Taos*, n.d., lithograph,
image 224 x 250 mm (8⁷/₈ x 9⁷/₈ in), printer unknown.
Collection, Mr. and Mrs. Van Deren Coke, Santa Fe

4 Gerald Cassidy (1869–1934), *Portrait of Mrs. M.*, 1916, lithograph, sheet 569 x 398 mm
(22½ x 15¾ in), printed by Latham Litho and Printing Co., New York. Collection,
University Art Museum, University of New Mexico, Albuquerque, gift of Ina Sizer Cassidy
[45.10]

5 Gerald Cassidy (1869–1934), *Sand Storm*, ca. 1920, lithograph, image 255 x 348 mm
(10^1/$_{16}$ x 13^3/$_4$ in), printed by the artist. Collection, University Art Museum, University of
New Mexico, Albuquerque, gift of Ina Sizer Cassidy [45.15]

6 Ralph Pearson (1883–1958), *Church at Ranchos de Taos*, 1919, etching,
image 111 x 171 mm (4³/₈ x 6³/₄ in), printed by the artist. Collection, Museum of
Fine Arts, Museum of New Mexico, Santa Fe, gift of the artist [485]

Among dated prints in the collection of the Museum of Fine Arts,[13] the earliest made in the state are an etching by Pearson and a lithograph by Sandzen, both from 1919.[14] Though reflective of Pearson's modernist orientation only in its verve and freshness, his *Church at Ranchos de Taos* achieves a monumentality quite beyond its tiny size. Sandzen's transfer lithograph *Gran Quivira* echoes the drawings of Van Gogh in the vigor with which the soft, blunt crayon captures the gnarled forms of the junipers against the cloud-filled sky. Very likely, Sandzen took his transfer drawing from New Mexico to Wichita and had it printed there.[15]

IT WAS THE INTENTION of the Association of American Painters and Sculptors—the committee of twenty-five artists who organized the Armory Show—to open doors and minds: to "mark the starting point of the new spirit in art."[16]

8

7 Birger Sandzen (1871–1954), *Gran Quivira*, 1919, transfer lithograph,
image 402 x 552 mm (15^{13}/$_{16}$ x 21^{3}/$_{4}$ in), probably printed by Western Lithographic
Company, Wichita, Kansas. Collection, Museum of Fine Arts, Museum of New Mexico,
Santa Fe, gift of the artist and Mr. Carl J. Smalley [656]

Prominent among these artists were members of "The Eight,"[17] who, as a consequence of their commitment to a realistic and forthright depiction of daily life—including life in the slums of Manhattan—were called "the Ash Can school." The rejection of such subject matter as "anti-aesthetic" by the established academies led them to a vigorous advocacy of open-door exhibitions, to sponsorship of the first Independent Artists' Exhibition of 1910, and organization of the Armory Show.

It was this spirit that Robert Henri, the spiritual leader of The Eight, brought to Santa Fe in 1916. Henri's visits to New Mexico had substantial effect. Upon his advice, a policy of open exhibitions was adopted when the Museum of Fine Arts opened in November 1917. "[Henri's] dashing brushwork, aura of international travel, and convincing quality as a teacher combined to give him a degree of leadership among the painters in Santa Fe, and to some extent, even in Taos"[18] (in 1918 he was elected to associate membership in the Taos Society of Artists); and his influence was reinforced in subsequent years as other artists in his circle—George Bellows, Leon Kroll, John Sloan, and Randall Davey—came to Santa Fe.[19]

Bellows and Kroll stayed only briefly, but Davey became a permanent resident and Sloan returned summer after summer, almost every year until his death in 1951. As the best known painter-printmaker who had yet come to New Mexico, Sloan's presence did much to establish printmaking as a legitimate activity for artists. He had made his first etching in 1888, and by 1919, when accompanied by Davey and their wives he drove cross-country from New York in an open touring car, he had completed about two hundred etchings and lithographs. His first print of a western subject—a group of Hopi dancers, closely watched by observers—was based on a drawing done during the summer of 1919 or 1920; the lithograph was then printed by artist-lithographer Bolton Brown in New York. Davey's etching, *Penitentes*, is more evocative: a view of a ceremony that had great meaning for its participants, held in the light of lanterns and the crescent moon.

Both Sloan and Bellows were active members in the Painter-Gravers of America. Bellows created the most significant body of lithographs made by any American artist in the first quarter of the twentieth century. The single lithograph that resulted from his stay in Santa Fe during the summer of 1917 thus provides an interesting footnote to history. He traveled first to California, then to New Mexico, where he was given a studio at the Palace of the Governors. While in Santa Fe, he completed a number of works, among them a

8

9

10

8 John Sloan (1871–1951), *Hopi Snake Dance, Walpi Mesa,* 1922 [Morse 203], lithograph, image 326 x 237 mm (12⁷/₈ x 9³/₈ in), printed by Bolton Brown, New York. Collection, Tamarind Institute, Albuquerque, on extended loan to University Art Museum, University of New Mexico, Albuquerque

This impression is signed, titled, and dated by the artist in pencil, and is signed by the printer Bolton Brown. In Peter Morse's catalogue of Sloan's prints, the title is given as *Snake Dance* and the date as 1921.

9 Randall Davey (1887–1964), *Penitentes*, 1921, etching, image 122 x 178 mm
(4¹³/₁₆ x 7 in), printer unknown. Collection, Museum of Fine Arts, Museum of New Mexico,
Santa Fe, gift of the artist [559]

drawing and a painting of a subject alternatively titled *Road to Quevado* or
Well at Quevado; the drawing later served as a study for the lithograph *Well
at Quevado* [*sic*], probably drawn on stone in 1918 and printed in New York.²⁰

Also a member of the Painter-Gravers of America, though not in Henri's
circle, was the Swedish-American painter B. J. O. Nordfeldt, an accomplished
etcher and maker of color woodcuts, who upon a visit to Santa Fe, decided
to remain there. Nordfeldt had first studied at the Art Institute of Chicago,
then at the Académie Julian in Paris, and with the English artist Frank Morley
Fletcher, from whom he learned the intricate techniques of the traditional
Japanese woodcut.²¹ "As early as 1906 his wood-block prints were awarded
a Silver Medal at the International Print Exhibition in Milan. A Silver Medal

10

11

12

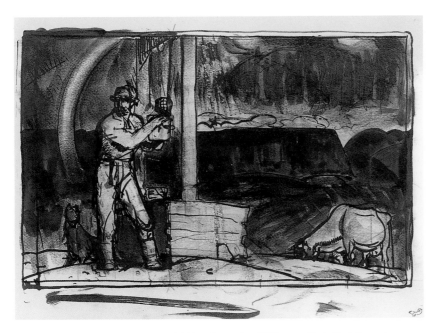

10 George Bellows (1882–1925), *Well at Quevado*, 1917, pencil, india ink, and crayon, image 259 x 401 mm (10³/₁₆ x 15³/₄ in). Collection, Print Department, Boston Public Library

11 George Bellows (1882–1925), *Well at Quevado*, ca. 1917–19 [Bellows 187; Mason 70], lithograph, image 245 x 353 mm (9⁵/₈ x 13⁷/₈ in), printer unknown. Collection, Print Department, Boston Public Library

12 B. J. O. Nordfeldt (1878–1955), *Man with Cane (Alvino Ortega)*, ca. 1925, etching, image 216 x 191 mm (8¹/₂ x 7¹/₂ in), printed by the artist. Collection, Museum of Fine Arts, Museum of New Mexico, Santa Fe, gift of Emily Abbott Nordfeldt [587]

13 B. J. O. Nordfeldt (1878–1955), *Crucifixion*, ca. 1925, etching with drypoint, image 190 x 251 mm (7¹/₂ x 9⁷/₈ in), printed by the artist. Collection, University Art Museum, University of New Mexico, Albuquerque, gift of Emily Abbott Nordfeldt [67.224]

was presented to him for an etching at the Panama-Pacific International Exposition in San Francisco in 1915. Similar recognition was accorded his etchings made in Santa Fe which can now be seen to be his best work in this medium."[22]

In his *Man with Cane (Alvino Ortega)*, one of a series of etched portraits of Hispanic men and women, we sense the reality of the relationship between the artist and his subject. It is clear that, like Cézanne, Nordfeldt saw his model in formal terms; equally evident, however, is the bond between the two men, one of mutual regard. In his drypoints of the Penitente rituals, Nordfeldt, like Davey, depicted the events with sympathy and respect.

12

13

15

An experienced etcher, Nordfeldt took pleasure in printing his own work. "He received a real thrill in doing them," Raymond Jonson said. "To see him etch a plate and especially the inking and printing was a real pleasure, for every move appeared in rhythm and in harmony with the materials."[23] But for many other artists, the fact that professional printers were unavailable in New Mexico profoundly affected their work. One must suspect that Sloan might have made more prints during his summers in Santa Fe if his printers, Ernest Roth and Peter Platt, had been close at hand rather than in New York; similarly, Cassidy, whose printers were in Brooklyn; and Hennings, whose printers were in Chicago.

Use of the lithographic medium was particularly affected by such distances. Many artists printed their own etchings and woodcuts, but few were able to print their lithographs, preferring to work with professional printers. As such printers were not available to them in New Mexico, artists sometimes went to Wichita, Kansas, where Birger Sandzen had been making prints since 1916. When Sandzen's former student C. A. Seward became art director of the Western Lithographic Company in 1923, he led the company into the business of printing for artists.[24] It was with Seward's encouragement that the young Kansas artist William Dickerson went to the Art Institute of Chicago in 1930 to study lithography with Bolton Brown; subsequently, Dickerson returned to Wichita and printed for artists from stone. Wichita thus became one of the few places in the United States where printing both from plates and stones was available. Dickerson often visited New Mexico during the summer months, and many of his lithographs are of New Mexican subjects.

GUSTAVE BAUMANN, who, like Nordfeldt, was a pioneer of the color woodcut in America, had studied at the Art Institute of Chicago where among fellow students he met Ufer, Victor Higgins, and E. Martin Hennings. Beginning in 1918, Baumann was in Santa Fe for most of four years, during which his "talent and skill came to full flower: the brilliant simplicity and subtlety of color in the surrounding landscape inspired him to become an innovator and an acknowledged master of his art. . . . The hot, clear sunlight, the forested mountains, the dancing Indians, the lilacs of Spring, and the October aspens were, in a sense, first perceived by him."[25] The fluid contours and massed forms of *San Geronimo—Taos*, one in a series of richly complex color woodcuts Baumann made between 1918 and 1922, reflects his study in Munich and his encounter with *Jugendstil*; simultaneously, the luminous color proclaims

CHURCH AT CANYONCITO   Wm Dickerson

14 William Dickerson (1904–72), *Church at Canyoncito*, 1942, lithograph,
image 220 x 302 mm (8¹¹/₁₆ x 11¹⁵/₁₆ in), printed by George C. Miller, New York.
Collection, University Art Museum, University of New Mexico, Albuquerque, gift of the
Friends of Art [79.421]

his joyous response to a new environment. "In a deceptive sense the woodblock
art of Baumann is an art of place, with its affectionate, sometimes vibrant,
recording of a particular curve in a river's movement, a particular moment
in a perspective of a mountain or desert road, a particular portion of a garden's
growth."[26] Always, it speaks in color and in a language of forms. Throughout
his long life as a working artist, during which he completed nearly two hundred
color woodcuts, Baumann retained an openness to stylistic directions other

Plate I

17

than his own; he had a "curiosity of spirit" that led to him to admire the work of Paul Klee and, in later years, to visit Max Ernst in Sedona.[27]

Other artists came to New Mexico in the 1920s, and with them a significant increase in printmaking. E. Martin Hennings, who first visited Taos in 1917 and moved there in 1921, made both etchings and lithographs in the early and mid-1920s. The accomplished Dutch artist Henry C. Balink also visited New Mexico in 1917, where in November of that year his work was shown in the inaugural exhibition at the Museum of Fine Arts; after returning to Holland in 1919, he came back to Santa Fe in 1924 and became, according to his own description, "one of the first resident etchers."[28] Josef A. Imhof, who had once worked as a lithographer for Currier and Ives, lived in Albuquerque from 1906 to 1912; after a long absence, he returned to New Mexico in 1929, this time to Taos, where he was probably the first artist to have a lithograph press.

Though the prints of Hennings, Balink, and Imhof are similar in subject and share a spirit of respect for the "intricate blend of traditional values and spiritual concerns" which the Pueblo culture represents,[29] they differ in style and character. While drawn with a crisp, cool eye, Hennings's *Stringing the Bow* retains more than an echo of the romantic sentimentality with which he (and other Anglo artists) viewed the native American.[30] Balink is more the realist; he refuses to idealize *Chief Pacanneh*, but instead presents a straightforward and dignified portrait without editorial comment. Imhof, who prided himself on factual authenticity, nonetheless endows *Geronimo of Taos* with a dramatic haughtiness that perhaps reflects as much the temperament of the artist as that of the man portrayed.

By contrast, when John Sloan turned his eye upon the intersection of cultures in New Mexico, he did so with caustic wit. In *Indian Detour* he depicts an Indian dance all but obliterated by tourists and their buses; in his satirical *Knees and Aborigines*, he portrays a "civilized audience when skirts were at their height viewing the more modestly dressed savages at a Pueblo Indian dance in New Mexico. Perhaps," Sloan concludes, "the pun may be permitted."[31]

But Sloan was alone in such irreverence. Will Shuster, who learned etching from Sloan, viewed the Pueblo culture with a more typical warmth and sympathy, and created many memorable images of Pueblo life and ceremonies on the copper plate. Shuster was one of five painters who had come to Santa Fe in 1919 and 1920, and who, under the leadership of Josef Bakos, had formed an artist's group called Los Cinco Pintores.[32] Although they saw themselves

15

16

17

18

20

18

15 E. Martin Hennings (1886–1956), *Stringing the Bow*, ca. 1925–26, etching,
image 203 x 254 mm (8 x 10 in), posthumous impression, printed in 1977. Collection,
Museum of Fine Arts, Museum of New Mexico, Santa Fe, gift of Mr. and Mrs. Robert R.
White [86.543.4]

16 Henry Balink (1882–1963), *Chief Paccaneh*, ca. 1927, etching, image 144 x 97 mm
($5^{11}/_{16}$ x $3^{13}/_{16}$ in), printed by the artist. Collection, Museum of Fine Arts, Museum of New
Mexico, Santa Fe, gift of the estate of William C. Ilfeld [2192b]

17 Josef Imhof (1871–1955), *Geronimo of Taos, N.M.*, n.d., lithograph,
image 349 x 200 mm (13³/₄ x 7⁷/₈ in), printed by the artist. Collection, Museum of Fine
Arts, Museum of New Mexico, Santa Fe, gift of the artist [129]

18 John Sloan (1871–1951), *Knees and Aborigines*, 1927 [Morse 230], etching, image 178 x 152 mm (7 x 6 in), printed by Ernest Roth, New York. Collection, Museum of Fine Arts, Museum of New Mexico, Santa Fe, gift of Ann L. Maytag [84.76.15]

as an avant-garde, their rebellion against the academy was founded more in social than in formal principles, a fact that often resulted in an uneasy tension between the realist and modernist elements in their work. Among the five painters, Willard Nash was the most directly influenced by Cubism, as is seen in his lithograph *Crossbearer*, where the buildings at the right (reminiscent of Picasso's drawings in the Catalan town of Horta) provide an odd contrast to the figures of the Penitentes. Nash made a number of lithographs and printed most of them himself in very small editions.[33]

19

19 Willard Nash (1898–1943), *Crossbearer*, ca. 1930, lithograph, image 292 x 394 mm (11½ x 15½ in), printed by the artist. Collection, Mr. and Mrs. Van Deren Coke, Santa Fe

20 Will Shuster (1893–1969), *Prayer for the Hunt*, n.d., aquatint, image 178 x 225 mm (7 x 8⅞ in), printed by the artist. Collection, Museum of Fine Arts, Museum of New Mexico, Santa Fe [426]

CHAPTER 2

BEFORE AND DURING
THE GREAT DEPRESSION

Although GEORGIA O'KEEFFE has gained greater fame than has Andrew Dasburg, her work did not significantly influence younger artists in New Mexico. Dasburg's work, in that sense, was by far the more important. One of the first Americans seriously to explore the implications of Cubism and abstract art, Dasburg exhibited three paintings and a sculpture in the Armory Show; by the end of 1913 he was working in an abstract style closely related to the Synchromist paintings of his friend Morgan Russell. In that year Dasburg also formed a friendship with Mabel Dodge, whose "Thursday Evenings" were the New York equivalent of Gertrude Stein's Paris salons. Dasburg's relationship with Dodge (later Mabel Dodge Luhan) continued in the years that followed, and in 1918 she invited him to visit her in Taos.

Dodge became a "pivotal figure" in Taos "primarily because of the people she attracted . . . [either by] direct invitation or by her influence"[1]—Dasburg, O'Keeffe, and John Marin; Robinson Jeffers, Leo Stein (Gertrude's brother), Thornton Wilder, and Tennessee Williams; the Russian émigré Nicolai Fechin; and the psychologist Carl Jung. It was a heady mix.

Dasburg first came west in 1918, returned in 1920, and almost every year thereafter spent the summer months in Santa Fe or Taos. Although he made only two prints in these years—two woodcuts made at the behest of his friend, the poet Willard (Spud) Johnson, for publication in Johnson's magazine *The Laughing Horse*[2]—he stimulated printmaking in other, indirect ways.

A long-time resident of Woodstock, New York, Dasburg continued to teach classes there and in New York City. He was a teacher of great power and effectiveness, with the consequence that among his students several would

21 Andrew Dasburg (1887–1979), *Taos Pueblo I*, 1926 [Adams 1], woodcut,
image 150 x 102 mm (5⁷/₈ x 4 in), printed by John Sommers, 1978.
Collection, Earl Stroh, Taos

26

follow him to New Mexico. One of these was Kenneth M. Adams, who studied with Dasburg in the summers of 1919 and 1920. Before coming to Taos in 1924, Adams spent two years in France, painting the Provençal landscape in company with his friend Ward Lockwood. Adams later persuaded Lockwood to join him to New Mexico, where both became Dasburg's devoted followers.

Dasburg was now working in a style far less "radical" than the work he had done in Woodstock. Even so, by comparison with the romantic realism practiced by the conservative Taos painters, he was a modernist. Similarly, Fechin, who, though he worked in a style barely tinged by Post-Impressionism, was seen as an artist from another world. Born in Russia, a student of the realist painter Ilya Repin, and a virtuoso draftsman, Fechin made a small (but undetermined) number of lithographs—all drawn with ease and assurance. In such prints as the vivacious *Mexican Girl*, he achieves an uncommon charm and informality.

22

More aggressive as an advocate of modernist ideas was the painter Emil Bisttram, who in 1931 founded the Taos School of Art. By the mid-1930s Bisttram was painting in a manner closely related to the geometric style of Wassily Kandinsky. Although representational, his lithograph *Peace* may also reflect Kandinsky's concern for "the emotions and feelings of human beings" as expressed in art; certainly it reflects Bisttram's interest in the theories of dynamic symmetry developed by the theoretician Jay Hambidge.

23

DURING A VISIT TO TAOS after work in Wichita, B. J. O. Nordfeldt encouraged Adams to take up lithography. The youngest member of the Taos Society of Artists (and the last to be invited to join the society before it disbanded in 1927), Adams responded immediately to the medium, sometimes using it to restate motifs also developed in his paintings.[3] Influenced both by Cézanne and Dasburg, Adams characteristically cloaked abstract structure with representational form, shrugging off the judgments of modernist critics who disparaged his work as "academic," and of conservative critics who found it too "abstract." The technique of crayon lithography, which permitted him to build forms slowly and deliberately, was particularly congenial to Adams's formal manner; and he continued to work actively in the medium at intervals throughout his lifetime.[4]

24
25

It is likely that Nordfeldt also introduced Lockwood to lithography. The composition of Lockwood's *Taos Signs*, closely related to a painting, *Taos Plaza* (for which it served as a study), suggests that it was drawn in the fall of 1929, after the first of John Marin's summer visits to Taos, during which

26
27

27

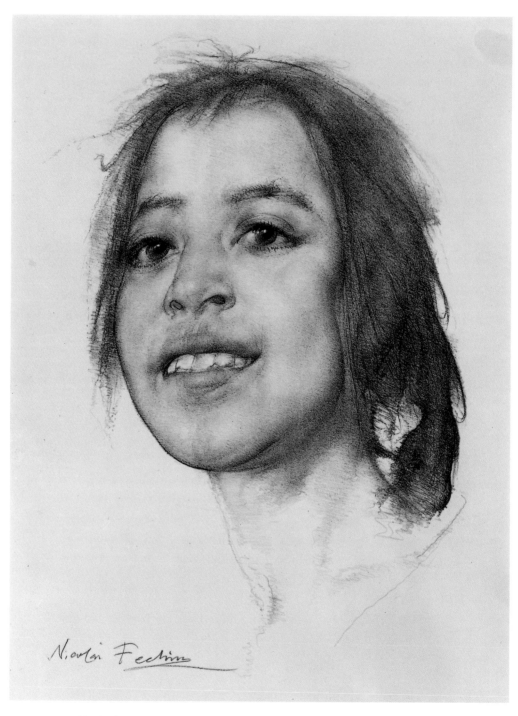

22 Nicolai Fechin (1881–1955), *Mexican Girl*, ca. 1940, lithograph, image 335 x 235 mm (13³/₄ x 9¹/₄ in), printed in Los Angeles, California; printer unknown. Collection, Tamarind Institute, on extended loan to University Art Museum, University of New Mexico, Albuquerque

28

23 Emil Bisttram (1895–1976), *Peace*, 1930, lithograph, image 203 x 203 mm (8 x 8 in),
printer unknown. Collection, Museum of Fine Arts, Museum of New Mexico, Santa Fe,
Vivian Sloan Fiske Bequest [4436]

24 Kenneth M. Adams (1897–1966), *Adobe Bricklayer*, 1934, lithograph,
image 234 x 249 mm (9^1/$_8$ x 9^{13}/$_{16}$ in), probably printed by George C. Miller, New York.
Collection, University Art Museum, University of New Mexico, Albuquerque, gift of
Lawrence O. Hogrefe [78.12]

25 Kenneth M. Adams (1897–1966), *Harvest*, 1940, lithograph, image 276 x 229 mm
(10⁷/₈ x 9 in), probably printed by George C. Miller, New York. Collection, Museum of Fine
Arts, Museum of New Mexico, Santa Fe, Vivian Sloan Fiske Bequest [4359]

31

26 Ward Lockwood (1894–1963), *Taos Signs*, 1929, lithograph, 318 x 406 mm (12¹/₂ x 16 in), probably printed at Western Lithographic Company, Wichita, Kansas. Ward and Clyde Lockwood Collection, Spencer Museum of Art, University of Kansas [72.406]

Dasburg and Lockwood had served as his guides to the better painting (and fishing) spots of the region.[5] Marin, like Dasburg, had been invited by Mabel Dodge Luhan to stay at her estate; and, again like Dasburg, his influence upon New Mexico's art and artists was substantial. Although a master etcher, Marin worked only in watercolor during his two summers in New Mexico (1929 and 1930).

IN 1926, THE EDITORS of *Forum* were making plans to publish Willa Cather's *Death Comes to the Archbishop* in serial form. They commissioned Howard Cook, whose work had previously appeared in the magazine, to make some woodcuts in Santa Fe which "might be used not to illustrate the story but to suggest the atmosphere" of its locale.[6] Cook traveled to Santa Fe in the fall and made several woodcuts there before venturing north to Taos. What was to have been a short visit west became an extended stay: "For a romantic

27 Ward Lockwood (1894–1963), *Taos Plaza*, 1934?, oil on canvas, 622 x 750 mm
(24¹/₂ x 29¹/₂ in). Collection, University Art Museum, University of New Mexico,
Albuquerque, gift of Clyde Lockwood [64.63]

young artist," Cook wrote, ". . . here, long before tourism, was a living,
colorful, strange, appealing Indian and Spanish culture right in an exciting,
primitively beautiful part of our own country."[7] He remained in Taos through
the winter and in 1927 completed twenty-nine woodcuts and etchings.

Also in that year, Cook met Barbara Latham, a young artist who, after study
at the Art Students League and with Dasburg in Woodstock, had traveled
alone to Taos. She and Cook fell in love and were married: "The newly-weds
soon moved into a small outbuilding on the grounds of the Harwood home in
Taos (now the Harwood Foundation). Here Cook continued to work on his
woodblocks and early etchings. He had a small etching press bolted to a table
and operated by a crank handle which, he complained, frequently broke."[8]
Among the prints Cook completed that year were many of his most memorable
New Mexico subjects. These, together with drawings, were exhibited at the
Museum of Fine Arts in Santa Fe, early in 1928.

28
29

33

28 Howard Cook (1901–80), *Morning Smokes, Taos Pueblo,* 1927 [Duffy 50], woodcut,
image 204 x 204 mm (8 x 8 in), printed by the artist. Collection, University Art Museum,
University of New Mexico, Albuquerque, gift of the artist [XO.44]

34

29 Howard Cook (1901–80), *The Lobo*, 1927 [Duffy 48], etching, image 100 x 151 mm
(4 x 6 in), printed by the artist. Collection, University Art Museum, University of New
Mexico, Albuquerque, gift of the artist [63.23]

The Cooks then drove cross-country to New York, in search of a market for
his work. Even in the late twenties, and even in New York, few commercial
art galleries were interested in exhibiting the work of American printmakers:
among those that did, one of the most important was the gallery established
by Erhard Weyhe in 1919 as an adjunct to his bookstore in New York. Carl
Zigrosser, the gallery's curator from 1919 to 1940 (and later curator of prints
at the Philadelphia Museum of Art) was a strong and effective supporter of
the artists he represented.

Zigrosser immediately responded to Cook's prints from New Mexico, which
probably triggered his decision to write Dasburg and make plans for a trip
west, first by train to Raton, thence by bus to Taos, where he was met by
Lockwood. (Zigrosser would describe the trip as a "memorable" discovery of

30 Mabel Dwight (1876–1955), *Cemetery*, 1929, lithograph, image 255 x 338 mm
(10 x 13³/₈ in), probably printed by George C. Miller, New York. Collection, Tamarind
Institute, on extended loan to University Art Museum, University of New Mexico,
Albuquerque

30   the Southwest.)[9] It is also likely that Cook's enthusiasm for Taos led other
gallery artists to visit New Mexico, including Mabel Dwight, whose lithograph
Cemetery was drawn in 1929.

    Zigrosser, who became Cook's lifelong friend, described his style as neither
"obvious nor flamboyant . . . the style of a trained observer and a skilled
technician, of a reserved but alert intelligence."[10] These qualities together
led Cook to a formal synthesis—particularly in his New York subjects of
1928–32—which quickly established his position in the front rank of American
printmakers.[11]

31   A similar synthesis, parallel to Cook's but different in spirit, is seen in
Barbara Latham's prints, also exhibited by Zigrosser at the Weyhe Gallery.
Both artists reflect in their work a commitment to the Precisionist spirit of
the 1920s, a spirit which Joshua Taylor has described as "a moral, almost a
religious creed" among American artists of that time.[12]

36

31 Barbara Latham (1896–1989), *The Rail*, ca. 1949, lithograph, image 235 x 324 mm (9¹/₄ x 12³/₄ in), printed by George C. Miller, New York. Collection, Museum of Fine Arts, Museum of New Mexico, Santa Fe, gift of Mr. and Mrs. Ford D. Good [2428]

THE STOCK MARKET CRASH that ended the 1920s had a delayed effect upon the artists of New Mexico. At first, Lockwood recalled, "The great depression was slow in making its effect evident in the rural community of Taos, but as the months passed by painters felt the blow as the art market practically disappeared."[13] For artists who depended, as most New Mexico artists did, upon sale of their work, the effect was drastic. Some left New Mexico in search of employment; those who remained faced a grim future.[14]Not until the second year of Franklin D. Roosevelt's New Deal was their loss of income compensated in some degree by new federal programs designed to provide assistance to art and artists.

When in 1933 the first of these programs, the Public Works of Art Project (PWAP), was established within the Treasury Department, the country was divided into sixteen regions; Santa Fe became the administrative headquarters of Region Thirteen, comprising Arizona and New Mexico, and the regional director, Jesse Nusbaum, lacking a background in art, appointed Gustave Baumann as area coordinator. It became his job to check on artists' progress "and to offer encouragement and motivation when needed. Baumann's reports to Nusbaum were unusually candid and direct," and, it should be added, strongly supportive of artists who, as he put it, thought "more of their work than of remuneration."[15]

While designed to give assistance to needy artists, the PWAP was selective in its employment; artists had to be competent. Once employed, they were generally given free choice in selection of media. When the PWAP ended in June 1934, it was followed by other projects, best known of which is the Federal Art Project of the Works Progress Administration (WPA/FAP). Because the WPA/FAP was a program intended primarily for economic relief, "regardless of the aesthetic result,"[16] not all of the artists employed by the PWAP could meet the financial criteria of the new program. On the other hand, artists who did not meet the PWAP's definition of professional competence were readily accepted by the WPA/FAP, with the consequence that their work ranged through all levels of quality. Foremost among the artists who made prints both for the PWAP and WPA/FAP in New Mexico were Nordfeldt, Adams, and Gene Kloss.

Originally from California but a resident of Taos since 1929, Kloss was by the 1930s already in full command of the complex copperplate processes—including etching, drypoint, aquatint, soft ground, and mezzotint—which she was to employ with sensitivity and skill for more than fifty years. Printed as a part of her work for the WPA/FAP, the rich and sensuous tonalities of *The Sanctuary, Chimayo* verify Baumann's judgment that Kloss, the "project's one etcher, [was] most intent on giving value for money received."[17] For Kloss, the drawing, the biting, and the printing of a plate were interdependent parts of a single process: "I want the finished print to enable the viewer to see the design, the subject matter from across the room, at arm's length or under a magnifying glass—also upside-down for satisfactory abstract design. . . . Art is life to me and is plastic thought. . . ."[18]

In some regions of the United States—particularly in and around New York—the WPA/FAP proved an important stimulus to American printmaking. In New Mexico, however, its effect was limited by the fact that none of the sixteen graphic workshops established by the WPA/FAP was located in a state between Illinois and California. Lacking access to a federally supported workshop, Kloss was fortunate in that her work for the projects coincided with her purchase of a large Sturges etching press. This, she recalls, "enabled me to

32

32 Gene Kloss (b. 1903), *The Sanctuary, Chimayo*, 1934 [Kloss 300], drypoint and
aquatint, image 356 x 254 mm (14 x 10 in), printed by the artist, Works Progress
Administration, Federal Art Project. Collection, Museum of Fine Arts, Museum of New
Mexico, Santa Fe [647]

do much larger plates than [had] the smaller presses I had owned previously.
. . . It was geared, had a big wheel to turn, and an old-fashioned letter presss
built in below which gave it stability and an ideal place for dampening paper,
weight 1080 lbs."[19] Kloss was, however, among the few who had adequate
press equipment, and one can only speculate as to the prints that might have
been made in New Mexico if a fully equipped graphics workshop had been
available to other artists who were working here.

In the absence of such a workshop, the screen print had many attractions.
Now more frequently called the serigraph—a term coined by Carl Zigrosser
in 1940 to separate "creative work" from "commercial" screen printing[20]—
the medium first found wide use as a fine arts medium in the print workshops
of the WPA/FAP. The Washington office then distributed technical information
to its regional directors; this, in New Mexico, came to Russell Vernon Hunter,
who called upon the Santa Fe artist Louie H. Ewing to explore its potential.
Because the screen print was less laborious than the woodcut and required
less equipment (and technical skill) than lithography, it was ideally adapted
to use in places that lacked fully equipped workshops. Although Ewing was
to become Santa Fe's most popular serigrapher, much of his work was overly
affected by the taste of the tourist trade.

BETWEEN 1929 AND 1938, Howard Cook made more than one hundred
prints, while receiving two Guggenheim fellowships and completing a series
of commissions to execute murals for public buildings. Then, in 1939, he
and Barbara "purchased their 'permanent' home in Talpa, just south of Taos.
A parade of visitors commenced including Yasuo Kuniyoshi and his wife,
Andrew Dasburg, the Jean Charlots, and Carl Zigrosser."[21] Some of the visitors
made prints that reflected their perceptions of Taos. Federico Castellón, who,
like Cook and Latham, exhibited at the Weyhe Gallery in New York, based
33   his evocative *Taos Tryst* on memories of his stay there. Ellison Hoover, a
34   master of the lithographic crayon, created a memorable vision of Taos Pueblo,
brightly lit by the sun beneath a soft grey sky. George Elbert Burr and Frederick
Monhoff, both noted etchers, made fine prints in and around Santa Fe: Burr
drew a number of romantic landscapes of the plains and mesas; Monhoff
vividly depicted Indian dances and ceremonies. Arnold Rönnebeck, for a time
director of the Denver Art Museum (and also a member of the Weyhe Gallery
35   circle), imposed an orderly geometry upon the hills and trees of *El Monte Sol,*
36   *Santa Fe;*[22] and the Washington printmaker Prentiss Taylor depicted an inviting
road to the mountains, overhung by heavy clouds.

40

33 Federico Castellón (1914–71), *Taos Tryst*, ca. 1942 [Freundlich 28], etching, image 197 x 302 mm (7³/₄ x 11⁷/₈ in), printed by the artist. Courtesy of the Syracuse University Art Collections [1967.955]

34 Ellison Hoover (1888–1955), *Untitled (Taos Pueblo)*, n.d., lithograph,
image 303 x 225 mm (12 x 8⅞ in), printed by George C. Miller, New York. Collection,
University Art Museum, University of New Mexico, Albuquerque, purchase, Julius
Rolshoven Memorial Fund [80.26]

42

35 Arnold Rönnebeck (1885–1947), *El Monte Sol, Santa Fe*, 1927, lithograph,
image 217 x 305 mm (8⁹/₁₆ x 12¹/₁₆ in), probably printed by George C. Miller, New York.
Collection, Tamarind Institute. On extended loan to University Art Museum, University of
New Mexico, Albuquerque [EL 82.1]

36 Prentiss Taylor (b. 1907), *Towards Santa Fe*, 1958, lithograph, image 299 x 405 mm
(11³/₄ x 15³/₄ in), printed by George C. Miller & Son, New York. Collection, University Art
Museum, University of New Mexico, Albuquerque, gift of the artist [84.92]

From Texas and Oklahoma came a steady stream of artists, some of whom
became summer residents. Beginning in 1927 Alexandre Hogue spent three
to seven months a year in Taos (he had made a first visit in 1920), where he
became a close friend of the Blumenschein family. Hogue, whose Taos summers ended with the coming of World War II, stayed aloof from disputes among
the Taoseño artists—a neutrality which bore fruit in 1936 and 1938 when
Josef Imhof (uncharacteristically) offered Hogue use of his lithograph press.
Hogue describes Imhof as a "loner" and "difficult to know," and believes that
he (Hogue) may have been "the only artist Imhof ever helped in Taos."²³
Perhaps the finest of Hogue's Taos lithographs is *Five Crosses* (1938), a striking
composition that provides a less familiar view of the often-painted church at
Ranchos de Taos. Also notable for their work in New Mexico were Texan
visitors Jerry Bywaters, an active printmaker who later became director of the
Dallas Museum of Fine Arts, and Loren Mozley from Austin.

37

44

"Five Crosses" 13/20

Alexandre Hogue 1938

37 Alexandre Hogue (b. 1898), *Five Crosses*, 1938 [DeLong 46], lithograph,
image 216 x 318 mm (8¹/₂ x 12¹/₂ in), printed by the artist. Jerry Bywaters Collection on
Art of the Southwest, Hamon Arts Library, Southern Methodist University, Dallas

CHAPTER 3

AFTER THE WAR

W HEN GENE BARO LOOKED BACK at thirty years of American printmaking, he saw 1947 as a "threshold year."[1] It was then that the Brooklyn Museum began its influential series of national exhibitions, that the artist Jean Charlot organized a historic retrospective of prints made in America during earlier decades, and that the art community—artists, critics, dealers, museums, and art schools—returned more or less to normal, following the disruptions of World War II.

The war had caused profound change in New Mexico, permanently altering the state's economy and its tempo of life. By its end, Albuquerque had more than doubled in population; the sleepy town of the 1930s had become a sprawling urban center, characterized, in Peter Walch's phrase, by a "messy vitality."[2] In printmaking, that vitality had been stimulated by the presence of Adja Yunkers.

Yunkers came to Albuquerque from Europe via New York. Born in Riga in 1900 (then a city in Czarist Russia and later the capital of Latvia), Yunkers had traveled widely—in Germany, Italy, Spain, Cuba, Mexico, and France—before taking wartime refuge in Sweden.[3] Following those dark years, he arrived in New York at a moment of intellectual and artistic ferment. The war had brought to New York many of the leading figures of the modern movement, some of whom Yunkers had known in Europe. Prominent among them was Stanley William Hayter, at whose printmaking studio, Atelier 17 (displaced from Paris in 1940), the Europeans met the Americans of the new avant-garde, the Abstract Expressionists. Yunkers found himself immediately at home: "History for me," he later said, "started with my landing in New York in 1947."[4]

Yunkers was a master of the color woodcut, a medium he used with rugged force in the technical tradition of Edvard Munch and the Expressionists of *Die Brücke,* some of whom Yunkers had known in Germany. It was a method that required the cutting of many blocks, the inking of each block in multiple colors, and extensive overprinting, often on tissue-like paper. The painterly quality of the prints so produced was the essential characteristic of the "wood-cut renaissance," a movement in which American artists had participated even before Yunkers's arrival.[5]

Though stimulated by the "exquisite intellectual pleasures" of New York, Yunkers nonetheless sought escape from the "cave dwellers" of the city.[6] Because his wife Kerstin suffered from severe asthma (and was expecting a child), they sought a warm, dry climate. The specific origin of Yunkers's interest in New Mexico is unknown, but Raymond Jonson was apparently instrumental in his appointment to teach at the University of New Mexico in the summer of 1948.[7]

Yunkers and Kerstin found a small place to live in Corrales; their daughter Nambita was born in June; and Yunkers made up his mind to stay in the West. "New Mexico has 'got me,'" he wrote, "so that I would like to live here for good."[8] Although he "responded strongly to the wildness of the desert country, its sudden storms, its heightened color intensities, its shifting forms, and broken vistas,"[9] his attraction to the West was as much romantic as visual, akin to Van Gogh's dreams of an art colony in Arles, or to Gauguin's search for an unspoiled world in the tropics.

During 1948 and 1949, while supported by a Guggenheim Fellowship, Yunkers worked productively in New York and New Mexico, cutting many blocks and printing many monotypes. It was likely during the summer of 1949, when he again taught at the University of New Mexico, that he began to discuss with his friends the publication of a magazine designed to "restore the hand to the printing art, and to project a collaboration between the graphic arts and poetry."[10]

Though rebuffed in an effort to secure a continuing faculty appointment at the university,[11] Yunkers nonetheless made plans to move permanently to New Mexico. He built a small adobe studio in Corrales, where his wife and child

38

48

38 Adja Yunkers (1900–1984), *Miss Ever-Ready*, 1952 [Brooklyn Museum 66B], from the portfolio of five prints published by Rio Grande Graphics, color woodcut, image 467 x 248 mm (18³/₈ x 9³/₄ in), printed by the artist. Collection, University Art Museum, University of New Mexico, Albuquerque, museum purchase [88.5.1]

39 Frederick O'Hara (1904–80), *Comanche Gap IV*, 1959, lithograph,
image 572 x 384 mm (22^1/$_2$ x 15^1/$_8$ in), printed by the artist. Collection, Museum of Fine
Arts, Museum of New Mexico, Santa Fe, gift of Mrs. Mary R. Louise O'Hara [80.22.15]

50

remained during the winter months while he returned to New York and made preparations to escape that "dreary anthill" and move permanently to New Mexico. "I'm counting the days for my departure," he wrote, "and definite farewell to the plush-lined ashcans of this magical city, full of catacombs and unheard of horrors."[12]

In Albuquerque, in the summer of 1950, Yunkers's magazine took form as a portfolio, *Prints in the Desert*. His associates in this venture included two of his former students at the university, Jack Garver and Robert Walters; several prominent writers, Kenneth Lash and Ramón Sender among them; and painter Frederick O'Hara.[13]

Plates
II III

Announced as Volume I, Number 1, and dated Autumn 1950, *Prints in the Desert* was to be "issued quarterly in a limited edition of 220 copies," at a price of fifteen dollars (or fifty-five dollars for four issues). Yunkers and O'Hara were realistic, however, in their expectations of success, admitting in a foreword that "depending on the echo" the publication "might survive its own birth." It did not; there was to be no second issue.

A second ambitious project, the publication of print portfolios by Rio Grande Graphics, had no greater success, despite the distinction of the artists who made the prints (Yunkers, Gabor Peterdi, and Seong Moy) and the curators who wrote the essays (John Palmer Leeper, William Lieberman, and Una Johnson). The Rio Grande Workshop—"A School of the Fine Arts, Adja Yunkers, Director"—in which Yunkers and Richard Diebenkorn, then a graduate student at the University of New Mexico, were to have taught classes, closed before it opened, provoking a session in court. Though in the latter instance Yunkers was consoled by a judgment against his sponsors, New Mexico lost its charm for him. His Corrales studio was twice flooded, destroying much of his work; his marriage to Kerstin ended; and he returned to New York.

With Yunkers's departure, O'Hara became the most significant avant-garde printmaker in New Mexico. Born in Canada, O'Hara had come to Albuquerque in 1941 after a long stay in Europe and a period as director of the Santa Barbara School of Fine Arts in California. In 1949, stimulated by Yunkers, he turned from painting to printmaking, first in a group of brilliant color woodcuts, among them *Garden of Folly, Series II*; then in such lithographs as *Comanche Gap IV*, a print remarkable both for its imagery and technical inventiveness. Making use of a then little-used method of image transposition,[14] O'Hara combined echos of prehistoric petroglyphs with a Klee-like sensibility to create a mysterious world entirely his own.

Plate IV
39

40 John Tatschl (1906–82), *Pieta*, ca. 1947, woodcut, image 394 x 572 mm
(15¹/₂ x 22¹/₂ in), printed by the artist. Collection, Museum of Fine Arts, Museum of New
Mexico, Santa Fe, gift of Mrs. Rayford W. Alley, Jr. [3074]

40

BEFORE AND AFTER YUNKERS'S BRIEF STAY in New Mexico, the UNM
art department offered classes in printmaking taught by John Tatschl, an
Austrian-born sculptor who joined the faculty in 1946. "One of the most
popular professors on campus . . . [Tatschl's] range of interests [and] his
articulate conversation," made him UNM's "resident European." His students
found him to be demanding but supportive, "insightful about, and towards,
his students."[15] Although in the fifties, Tatschl made a series of forceful
woodcuts, most on religious themes, his effectiveness as a teacher was later
diminished by an irascible rejection of much that younger artists considered
new and important.

Handicapped by an inadequate studio, the UNM printmaking program
remained peripheral to painting during the fifties—a period during which
Richard Diebenkorn (as a graduate student), Elaine de Kooning, Robert Mallary, and Agnes Martin gained the university a foremost position among the
nation's art departments.[16] Even so, through its inability (or unwillingness) to

52

41 Elmer Schooley (b. 1916), *Ravens Feeding in a Field*, 1959, lithograph,
image 305 x 403 mm (12 x 15⁷/₈ in), printed by the artist. Collection, Museum of Fine
Arts, Museum of New Mexico, Santa Fe, gift of Mr. and Mrs. Ford D. Good [2167]

make a place for Yunkers on its faculty, UNM missed an opportunity to gain
leadership in printmaking during a critical period when, stimulated by the
cumulative effect of the postwar explosion in enrollment, Hayter's Atelier 17,
and the woodcut renaissance, printmaking gained new importance in American
universities.

Curiously, the most experienced printmaker on the UNM faculty did not
teach printmaking. Alexander Masley, whose fine wood engravings and etchings had brought him acclaim in the 1930s, had come to Albuquerque in
1947 to found and chair a department of art education (separate from the
department of art). Masley, who had once studied with Hans Hoffman in
Munich, continued to paint but was not active as a printmaker in New Mexico.

Leadership in printmaking was instead provided by Highlands University,
when in 1947 Elmer Schooley was invited to join its faculty. After attending
the University of Colorado as an undergraduate, Schooley had studied painting
with Philip Guston and lithography with Max Ballinger at the University of

41

53

42 Elmer Schooley (b. 1916), *Garden Walk*, ca. 1962, woodcut, image 527 x 386 mm
(20³/₄ x 15³/₁₆ in), printed by the artist. Collection, Museum of Fine Arts, Museum of New
Mexico, Santa Fe, gift of the artist [2871]

Iowa, and had taught for a year at the New Mexico State Teachers College in Silver City (now Western New Mexico University) before moving to Las Vegas. Schooley and O'Hara quickly became good friends as they compared notes on lithographic practices, working together first in Las Vegas, then in O'Hara's Albuquerque studio. Schooley acknowledges his debt to O'Hara, both technically and in terms of "attitudes and ideas [which] were at least as important to me as Guston's."[17]

With limited resources—but unlimited perseverance and commitment—Schooley made the printmaking program at Highlands the strongest in the state (and one of the few places in America where lithography was competently taught during the 1950s). "We had one old beat up 19th century press," Schooley relates, but "we were the first press in New Mexico to print lithos for other artists.[18] Nobody had dreamed of Tamarind at that time."[19] Schooley's own work from the 1950s and 1960s concerned itself with aspects of nature, meticulously observed and lovingly depicted. The sparkling woodcut *Garden Walk* is but one of many fine works from these years. Though he modestly describes his progression as a movement of "lurches and staggers,"[20] his paintings have continued to gain power since his retirement from teaching in 1977.

Although with an interruption following Schooley's departure, instruction in printmaking was also offered in Silver City. Dorothy McCray, who joined the faculty at Western New Mexico College in 1948, became one of the state's foremost exponents of color lithography. McCray's work was remarkable both technically and aesthetically. In the mid-1950s, few American artists were printing complex, multicolor lithographs; few, even in New York or California, were working so knowledgeably within an Abstract Expressionist idiom. Her radiant *Par Coeur* predates by five years Sam Francis's first series of color lithographs, published in Switzerland in 1960.[21]

Equally remarkable was the series of large-scale serigraphs created by William Lumpkins between 1958 and 1961. As early as the 1930s, Lumpkins, a Santa Fe painter and architect, had made paintings that anticipated Abstract Expressionism, and in 1938 he had been among the founding members of the Transcendentalist Painting Group in Santa Fe, an association of painters who had as their aim "to carry painting beyond the appearance of the physical world, through new concepts of space, color, light and design, to imaginative realms that are idealistic and spiritual."[22] While working in La Jolla, California, in the late fifties, Lumpkins began to make serigraphs, a medium which, he felt, had been misused by artists who sought to make it do tricks—

42

Plate V

43

43 William Lumpkins (b. 1909), *Untitled*, 1958–61, serigraph, image 230 x 271.8 cm (90$^{1}/_{2}$ x 107 in), printed by the artist. Collection, Albuquerque Museum, gift of Norma Lumpkins [82.219]

"imitative effects of other mediums." He sought instead to "return to the serigraph its basic form wherein the final result, a direct expression, is the end not the means."[23] In their scale, complexity, and expressive force, the large serigraphs that Lumpkins completed in those years are quite without precedent.

MODERNIST PRINTMAKERS who worked in New Mexico during the postwar years were handicapped by the very limited opportunities that then existed for exhibition of their work. In Albuquerque, Raymond Jonson made available the space of his new gallery at UNM, but in Santa Fe the galleries—few in number by comparison with today—were devoted primarily to exhibition of "traditional" New Mexican paintings: "Cowboys and Indians," as Lumpkins describes them.[24] Even conservative prints received little attention. Although the Museum of New Mexico's "open door" policy had long permitted artists to exhibit prints in the annual Fiesta exhibitions, it was not until February 1947 that the Fine Arts Museum organized a group exhibition devoted solely to prints. This exhibition, which reflected, and undoubtedly encouraged, increased printmaking activity, became the first in a series of twelve annual exhibitions, the last of them held in 1959.[25] Because the third exhibition (1949) was smaller than its predecessors, the format was revised in 1950 to include drawings.[26]

As might be expected, these annual exhibitions included prints by many of the artists who had established themselves as New Mexico's leading printmakers in the years before the war: Adams, Baumann, Cook, Imhof, Kloss, Latham, Shuster, and Sloan. They were joined by McCray, O'Hara, Schooley, Tatschl, and, during his stay in New Mexico, by Yunkers.

Randall Davey, who traveled frequently to Colorado Springs for the polo games at the Broadmoor, exhibited new lithographs, printed by Lawrence Barrett, with whom he worked intermittently from the mid-1940s until about 1960. Davey's *Wet Day at the Track* is a typical product of the Davey-Barrett collaboration: skilled and sensuous in its exploration of the lithographic vocabulary; superficial, perhaps, but utterly elegant and charming.

The checklists of the museum's exhibitions reveal that the number of artists making prints in New Mexico remained quite small in the fifties. New arrivals during the 1940s had settled principally in Taos and Santa Fe, where a majority of the state's artists still lived and worked.[27] To Taos had come Oli Sihvonen, who had studied with Josef Albers at Black Mountain College in North Carolina; and Beatrice Mandelman, an abstract painter and printmaker who had

44

47

57

44 Randall Davey (1887–1964), *Wet Day at the Track*, ca. 1946, lithograph, image 270 x 355 mm (10⁵/₈ x 14 in), printed by Lawrence Barrett, Colorado Springs. Collection, University Art Museum, University of New Mexico, Albuquerque, gift of Mason Wells [69.78]

45 Agnes Tait (1894–1981), *Ritual on the Mesa*, 1944 [Peña 38], lithograph, image 354 x 438 (13¹/₈ x 17¹/₄ in), probably printed by George C. Miller & Son, New York. Collection, Museum of Fine Arts, Museum of New Mexico, Santa Fe, gift of the artist [275]

58

46 Ira Moskowitz (b. 1912), *Yei-bei-chi Masks*, 1946, lithograph, image 298 x 394 mm (11³/₄ x 15¹/₂ in), printer unknown. Collection, Museum of Fine Arts, Museum of New Mexico, Santa Fe, purchased with funds from the Museum of New Mexico Foundation [2136]

made color lithographs at the FAP workshop in New York. (Mandelman was also a founding member of the National Serigraph Society.) To Santa Fe had come Ira Moskowitz, who made a series of vigorously drawn black-and-white lithographs of Indian ceremonials during the mid-1940s;[28] Helen Farr, a painter and printmaker who had married John Sloan in 1944 following the death of his first wife Dolly; Agnes Tait, who had learned lithography in Paris while studying at the Ecole des Beaux-Arts and had continued to make lithographs in New York before coming to Santa Fe in 1941; Arthur W. Hall, a skilled etcher and frequent prize winner in national print exhibitions; and his wife Norma Bassett Hall, who made color woodcuts and serigraphs, and who was, like her husband, a charter member of the Prairie Print Makers.[29]

46

45

Print # IV 7/30   *Oli Sihvonen '49*

47 Oli Sihvonen (b. 1921), *Block Print IV*, 1949, woodcut, image 218 x 330 mm
(8³/₈ x 13 in), printed by the artist. Jonson Gallery Collection, University Art Museum,
University of New Mexico, Albuquerque, bequest of Raymond Jonson [82.221.1239]

From Albuquerque came lithographs by the calligrapher Ralph Douglass,
professor of art at UNM; modernist serigraphs by Robert Leland Kiley; and

48 fanciful engravings by Howard Schleeter, a talented artist who enjoyed the
(sometimes ambivalent) support of his friend Raymond Jonson. From Las Vegas
and Silver City came prints by artists who studied with Schooley or McCray.
From San Patricio came the lithographs of Peter Hurd, and from Carlsbad the
etchings and engravings of Roderick Mead.

Hurd, whose popularity as an artist reflected both his aesthetic and personal
ties to the Wyeth family, had begun to make lithographs in the 1930s before

49 moving to New Mexico. His print *The Night Watchman,* based on a drawing
done in Roswell, was drawn on stone in Philadelphia and printed by Theodore
Cuno, with whom Hurd continued to work for some years thereafter, sometimes
shipping stones to him but more often piling them into a horse trailer and

48 Howard Schleeter (1903–76), *Glow Bugs*, 1946, wood engraving, image 205 x 154 mm
(8¹/₈ x 6¹/₁₆ in), printed by the artist. Collection, University Art Museum, University of New
Mexico, Albuquerque, gift in memory of Jack L. Steinberg [85.59]

49 Peter Hurd (1904–84), *The Night Watchman*, 1935 [Meigs 10], lithograph,
image 303 x 275 mm (12 x 10⅞ in), printed by Theodore Cuno, Philadelphia. Collection,
University Art Museum, University of New Mexico, Albuquerque [78.276]

62

50 Theodore van Soelen (1890–1964), *The Cook*, 1952, lithograph, image 349 x 502 mm
(13³/₄ x 19³/₄ in), printed by Lynton R. Kistler, Los Angeles. Collection, Museum of Fine
Arts, Museum of New Mexico, Santa Fe, gift of Mr. and Mrs. Henry Dendahl in memory of
Maggie B. and Levi Dumbauld, Sr. [643]

hauling them east to be printed. Hurd and the Santa Fe artist Theodore Van
Soelen also worked with Lynton Kistler, who, like Miller in New York, was
prepared to ship grained stones to artists. Van Soelen's *The Cook*, one in a   *50*
series of lithographs that documented the life of the cowboy, was printed by
Kistler in 1952; others in the series were printed by Schooley in Las Vegas.
Some artists adapted well to remote collaborations, but others were frustrated
by their inability to make changes in the drawing on the stone. Ila McAfee,   *51*
the Taos painter whose lithographs were printed either by Schooley or Barrett,
has expressed a typical response to problems that result: "I did only eighteen
lithographs as I was disturbed by not being able to make improvements after
seeing the . . . [image] printed on white paper when I had drawn on gray
stone."³⁰ Helen Blumenschein, daughter of the Taos pioneer, may well have

51 Ila McAfee (b. 1897), *A Small Ranch ("At Evening Time")*, ca. 1948, lithograph,
image 254 x 354 mm (10 x 14¹/₈ in), probably printed by Elmer Schooley, Las Vegas, N.M.
Collection of Mr. and Mrs. Van Deren Coke, Santa Fe

encountered similar problems in the making of her nostalgic landscapes of
the Taos valley, most of which were printed by Miller.

By contrast with such artists as Hurd, Van Soelen, McAfee, and Blumenschein, Roderick Mead was a surrealist painter and engraver who had studied
first at the Art Students League and Yale School of Fine Arts, then with Hayter
at his original Atelier 17 in Paris, where he was influenced by André Masson
and Yves Tanguy. Mead moved to New Mexico in 1941 and took up residence
on a ranch outside of Carlsbad, continuing to paint and make prints. He
exhibited regularly in Santa Fe, won frequent prizes in the annual graphics
exhibitions, and elicited praise from Ina Sizer Cassidy for his ability to clarify
and intensify his meanings through the emotional language of art.[31]

52

53

52 Helen Blumenschein (1909–89), *Unititled (Ranchos de Taos)*, 1945, lithograph,
image 356 x 247 mm (14 x 9³/₄ in), probably printed by George C. Miller, New York.
Collection, University Art Museum, University of New Mexico, Albuquerque, purchase,
Julius Rolshoven Memorial Fund [84.6]

Although Mead's equal in skill, Doel Reed was much less sensitive to the artistic revolution that transformed the character of American art between 1945 and 1960. First as a summer visitor to Taos and after 1959 as a resident, Reed explored "the canyons and mountain villages of the Sangre de Cristo range"[32] in search of motifs. These he would later develop into immaculate aquatints in which velvety blacks and whites "gleam as chalk marks on coal."[33] Reed is seen at his most typical in *Adobe and Wild Plum*, a print made in 1964 on commission from the Museum of Fine Arts.

BY THE EARLY FIFTIES, the many derivative, "traditional" painters who worked in Santa Fe were increasingly insecure. They had long regarded the Museum of Fine Arts as their special preserve (with characteristic tact, John Sloan had called it the "little pond for tadpoles")[34] and were determined to protect their territory. As early as the 1920s, Sharyn Udall reports, the museum had been targeted by the editor of the *Santa Fe New Mexican*, E. Dana Johnson, for its support of "bolshevism" (i.e., modernism) in art; and its head, painter Sheldon Parsons, had been "dismissed under fire."[35] Now, thirty years later, challenged once again by the presence of modernist artists, and (perhaps more to the point) disturbed by the judgment expressed by Mitchell Wilder and others that Albuquerque had become "the center of things in New Mexico so far as the creative end of art is concerned,"[36] they responded by mounting a campaign against "radical" exhibitions.

Sensitive to the prevailing political climate (Joe McCarthy was riding high), the museum responded, beginning with the fifth exhibition of prints and drawings in 1952, by asking artists to "label" their work according to its stylistic category. But there was to be no truce in the battle between "traditionalists" and "modernists." Long resolved elsewhere, it survived anachronistically in New Mexico—culminating in May 1960, when the regents of the Museum of New Mexico suddenly fired Frederick Black, acting head of the Museum of Fine Arts.

Black had come to the museum at the invitation of Reginald Fisher after study at the University of New Mexico with Adams, Davey, Jonson, and Tatschl. Although an abstract painter and printmaker, he was an advocate of balance and moderation. "It would seem to be axiomatic today," he wrote, "that any art center . . . owes it to itself to participate as fully as it may in the national scheme of things and that any center which sacrifices this participation for the sake of regionalism is ultimately inviting all the hardships of provincialism."[37] Traditional art, he continued "is not hopelessly outmoded by the

54

55

66

53 Roderick Mead (1900–1971), *Summer Night*, n.d., etching, image 227 x 449 mm (8¹⁵/₁₆ x 17¹¹/₁₆ in), printed by the artist. Collection, Roswell Museum and Art Center, purchase, Acquisitions Fund [74.5.4]

54 Doel Reed (1894–1985), *Adobe and Wild Plum*, 1965, etching and aquatint, image 305 x 470 mm (12 x 18½ in), printed by the artist. Collection, Museum of Fine Arts, Museum of New Mexico, Santa Fe, gift of the artist [1853]

55 Frederick Black (b. 1924), *Regatta: The Start*, 1953, color woodcut, image 279 x 425 mm (11 x 16³/₄ in), printed by the artist. Courtesy of the artist

various types of modernism. But neither should it be held that so-called modern art is but some fad or a thing soon to pass. . . ."[38]

Such moderation provided Black no protection. Apparently motivated by controversy centering on a 1959 exhibition (and on recommendation of a subcommittee headed by Peter Hurd) the regents acted to dismiss him; and in the process provoked a storm of protest. Garver and O'Hara cancelled their scheduled exhibitions at the museum; current exhibitors sought to remove their works from the walls; Artist's Equity protested; and distinguished artists—including Baumann, Dasburg, Davey, Jonson, and Schooley (among many others)—wrote in Black's behalf. It was all to no avail. Black resigned, as did two curators.[39] Although the annual printmaking exhibitions had not been at the center of the controversy, the series ended with Black's departure.

It was a sad end to a decade which had begun with such promise for printmaking in New Mexico. Dore Ashton, who had witnessed the ambitious beginnings at Adja Yunkers's invitation, wrote retrospectively in 1989 of the mysterious ways in which things happen and of the "surge of creative energy [which] eventually abated" and of "the unregenerate biases . . . [that] put unending obstacles in the way of art."[40]

The writer Edward Abbey, later to become a specialist in the activities of monkey-wrench gangs, called it just "another step backward for the arts in New Mexico. Mediocrity wins again."[41]

1 Gustave Baumann (1881–1971), *Morning Sun*, n.d., color woodcut, image 266 x 240 mm (10¹/₂ x 9¹/₂ in), printed by the artist. Collection, University Art Museum, University of New Mexico, Albuquerque [X0.310]

II Adja Yunkers (1900–1984), *Succubae*, 1950 [Brooklyn Museum 54], from the portfolio
Prints in the Desert, color woodcut, image 394 x 192 mm (15^1/$_2$ x 7^9/$_{16}$ in), printed by the
artist. Collection, Museum of Fine Arts, Museum of New Mexico, Santa Fe, gift of the artist
[1753b]

III Robert Walters (b. 1925), *Whorlworm*, 1950, from the portfolio *Prints in the Desert*, color woodcut, image 178 x 254 mm (7 x 10 in), printed by the artist. Jonson Gallery Collection, University Art Museum, University of New Mexico, Albuquerque, bequest of Raymond Jonson [82.221.1690.5]

IV Frederick O'Hara (1904–80), *Garden of Folly, Series II*, 1954, color woodcut, image 645 x 432 mm (25³/₈ x 17 in), printed by the artist. Collection, Museum of Fine Arts, Museum of New Mexico, Santa Fe, gift of Mrs. Mary R. Louise O'Hara [80.22.73]

V Dorothy McCray (b. 1915), *Par Coeur*, 1955, color lithograph, image 356 x 457 mm
(14 x 18 in), printed by the artist. Collection, Museum of Fine Arts, Museum of New
Mexico, Santa Fe, purchase, museum funds from the 1956 Annual Graphics Exhibition [74]

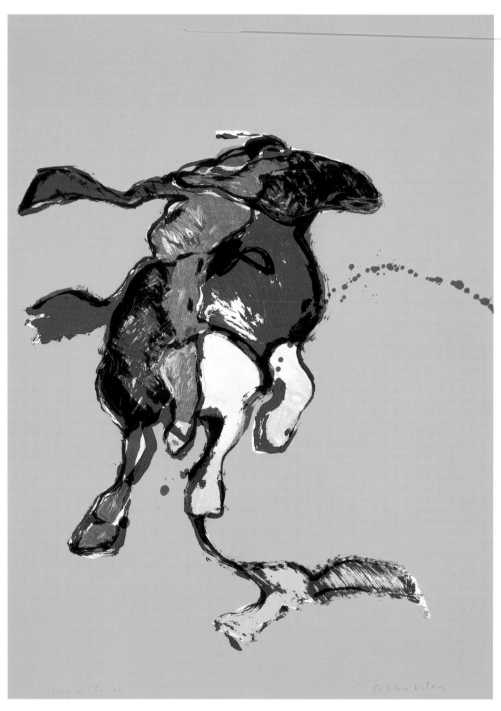

VI Fritz Scholder (b. 1927), *Indian on Galloping Horse after Remington #2 (First State)*, 1976 [Tamarind 76–645], color lithograph, image and sheet 762 x 559 mm (30 x 22 in), printed by Lynn Baker. Collection, Museum of Fine Arts, Museum of New Mexico, Santa Fe, gift of Mr. and Mrs. Ben Q. Adams [79.65.2]

VII Earl Stroh (b. 1924), *Symbiosis I*, 1979, color lithograph, image 466 x 635 mm
(18³/₈ x 25 in), printed by Lynn Baker at Southwest Graphics, Scottsdale, Arizona.
Collection, Museum of Fine Arts, Museum of New Mexico, Santa Fe, gift of Susan C.
Herter [87.106.1]

VIII Kenneth Price (b. 1935), *Untitled*, 1977 [Tamarind 77–103], color lithograph, image 662 x 489 mm (26 x 19¼ in), printed by William Masi. Tamarind Collection, University Art Museum, University of New Mexico, Albuquerque

TAMARIND:
LOS ANGELES TO ALBUQUERQUE

AMONG THE NEW GENERATION of American painters—the Abstract Expressionist avant-garde of the 1940s and 1950s—few made prints, and many were prejudiced against "an activity which they identified with ideas and methods completely foreign to their work."[1] As Franz Kline put it, "Printmaking concerns social attitudes, you know—politics and a public . . . like the Mexicans in the 1930s; printing, multiplying, educating; I can't think about it. I'm involved with the private image."[2] As a consequence of these perceptions, which were widely shared, most American prints in the 1950s were made by specialist-printmakers, not by painters.

Social attitudes aside, painter-printmakers characteristically require the support of printmaking studios, which in the postwar years declined substantially in number. The sixteen graphic workshops which had been maintained by the Federal Art Project during the 1930s had long been closed. Stanley William Hayter's Atelier 17, which had so stimulated artists in New York during the late 1940s, no longer benefited from Hayter's presence. Theodore Cuno, who had printed Peter Hurd's lithographs in Philadelphia, died in the mid-1950s; Lynton Kistler did little printing from stone after 1956; Lawrence Barrett's last work for an artist in Colorado Springs (a collaboration with Randall Davey) may have been in 1960. Clearly, if painter-printmaking was to continue in the United States, new workshops were required.

By the end of the 1950s, the postwar growth of intaglio printmaking programs in American art schools and universities had largely run its course.[3] Specialist-printmakers working in the tradition of Mauricio Lasansky and Gabor Peterdi were teaching in most institutions from coast to coast,[4] but while the prints made within this tradition were of high technical quality, most were reflections of a new academy, stylistically isolated from the principal currents of American art. Whatever the accomplishments of the specialist-printmakers during this period, their separation from the concerns of painting caused a loss of creative force.

American lithography had been stimulated during the 1950s by an important series of biennial exhibitions at the Cincinnati Art Museum,[5] but, even so, "there was little interest in lithography among the new generation of artists in New York,"[6] and it was taught in few schools across the country. (The instruction offered in New Mexico by Schooley and McCray was unusual at the time.)

The first efforts toward creation of a new environment were made in New York by Margaret Lowengrund, who established a printmaking workshop called The Contemporaries Graphic Art Centre in 1955; and by Tatyana Grosman, who soon thereafter began a print-publishing program, ambitiously titled Universal Limited Art Editions (ULAE).[7] These developments notwithstanding, it was evident that American printmaking could not enter a new era—and, specifically, that lithography could not survive—unless artists could find printers.

In Los Angeles, June Wayne conceived the idea that it might somehow be possible to establish a printmaking workshop which would have as its objectives "to create a pool of master-printers in the United States [and] to develop American artists, working in diverse styles, into masters of the medium."[8] In 1959 she made a formal proposal to the Ford Foundation for establishment of such a workshop; subsequently, the foundation made a grant for that purpose, and in 1960 Tamarind Lithography Workshop (TLW) opened its doors on a side street in Hollywood, California—on Tamarind Avenue, hence the name of the workshop.[9] I joined Wayne as Tamarind's associate director;[10] Garo Antreasian came from Indianapolis to become its first master printer.[11] Wayne and I had known one another since 1948, when we met at the Los Angeles studio of Lynton Kistler, who printed our lithographs for us; Antreasian was an experienced artist-lithographer who had taught since 1948 at the John Herron School of Art in Indianapolis.

We began to print for artists in July 1960, and by the following summer had completed well over two hundred editions for some of America's leading artists, among them three who had at one time worked in New Mexico: Adja Yunkers, Richard Diebenkorn, and Frederick O'Hara. Yunkers and Dieben-

72

korn received Tamarind fellowships; O'Hara came to the workshop at Antreasian's suggestion to demonstrate the process of image transposition with which he had continued to work in his Albuquerque studio.

At the end of Tamarind's first year, I accepted an appointment as dean of the College of Fine Arts at the University of New Mexico,[12] which, under the leadership of President Tom L. Popejoy, was then moving toward construction of an ambitious fine arts center. Perhaps because my predecessors as dean had been musicians, plans for an art gallery were tentative and incomplete. The art department was drifting; Raymond Jonson had retired, and the momentum of the fifties had been lost.

With the help of Mitchell Wilder, director of the Amon Carter Museum of Western Art in Fort Worth, we finished planning of the art gallery (later to become the University Art Museum), appointed Van Deren Coke as its director, and began organization of an inaugural exhibition: "Taos and Santa Fe: The Artist's Environment, 1882–1942." As Coke and I visited artists, I met few who made prints. Ward Lockwood, who had reestablished his residence in Ranchos de Taos after many years away (while teaching in Texas and California), was excited by his recent discovery of the collograph; but others— among them Howard Cook—spoke of printmaking as a past accomplishment: something over and done with. When the exhibition opened in 1963, it included only seven prints (by Baumann, Cook, Imhof, and Kloss).

It seemed clear that if New Mexico's artists were to participate in the revival of artist's printmaking, the university must assume leadership. In 1963 we invited Garo Antreasian (who had then returned to his teaching position in Indianapolis) to join the UNM faculty, and in 1965 we established an initial program of instruction for Tamarind printer-fellows at the university,[13] simultaneously creating an opportunity for New Mexico artists to make lithographs in collaboration with the printer-fellows we were training; in effect, the UNM workshop became a small "branch" of TLW.

In April, Raymond Jonson was the first artist invited to participate in this new program. Jonson had used lithograph crayons to make a number of fine drawings in the 1920s, but had had no opportunity to draw on stone at that time. One has only to look at these drawings to envision what Jonson might have accomplished as a printmaker in different circumstances. But by 1965 it was too late to engage Jonson's continuing interest: he made only three Tamarind editions, two of them in color. They were to be his only prints.

In June, Kenneth Adams drew his last stone, *Taos Indian;* he died the

56

57

58

56 Ward Lockwood (1894–1963), *Target*, ca. 1962, collograph, image 598 x 448 mm
(23¹/₂ x 17⁵/₈ in), probably printed by the artist. Collection, University Art Museum,
University of New Mexico, Albuquerque, gift of Barbara Ellis and Robert M. Ellis [77.213]

74

57 Raymond Jonson (1891–1982), *Sanctuario*, 1927, lithograph crayon on paper, image 292 x 413 mm (11$^{1}/_{2}$ x 16$^{1}/_{4}$ in). Collection, Museum of Fine Arts, Museum of New Mexico, Santa Fe, gift of Arthur Johnson [3215/23D]

following year. Among other artists who made prints at UNM during the 1960s (either under Tamarind auspices or as workshop projects) were faculty members Robert M. Ellis, Ronald Grow, Charles Mattox, and Alfred Young; and the expressionist painter Enrique Montenegro.

59

60

Tamarind's success in stimulating collaborative printmaking during the 1960s far exceeded our expectations. By the end of the decade new workshops staffed by Tamarind-trained printers had been established in a number of cities across the country.[14] In 1969 a decision was made to move Tamarind's workshop from Los Angeles to Albuquerque, and in 1970, with the assistance

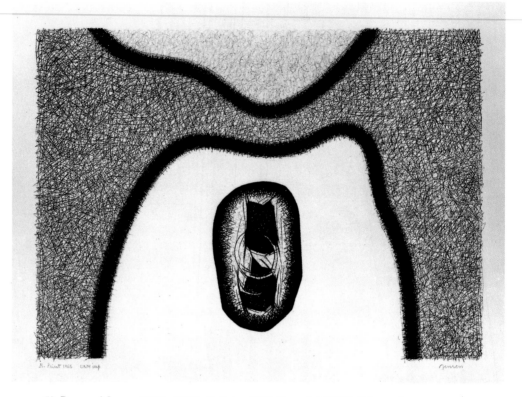

58 Raymond Jonson (1891–1982), *B. Print*, 1965 [Tamarind 1305], lithograph,
image and sheet 381 x 508 mm (15 x 20 in), printed by John Beckley. Tamarind Collection,
University Art Museum, University of New Mexico, Albuquerque

61

of a further grant from the Ford Foundation, Tamarind Institute was established
as a division of UNM's College of Fine Arts.[15] The university purchased a
vacant warehouse adjacent to the campus and, under Garo Antreasian's direction, remodeled it to meet our needs. Because this took some time, we
made use of the art department's workshop during the summer of 1970, and
it was there that the institute's work began. My lithograph *Strata* was the first
to be printed as a Tamarind Institute edition.

In the fall, when we moved into our permanent quarters, three presses were
on hand (the space was designed to accommodate six). Of the six printers,
three—including studio manager John Sommers—had come from Los Angeles,
and three had joined the program in New Mexico.[16]

While Tamarind had been in California, its substantial grant from the Ford
Foundation made it possible to offer fellowships to artists. All work was by

59 Alfred Young (b. 1936), *Sandia*, 1966, color lithograph, image and sheet 507 x 380 mm (20 x 15 in), printer unknown. Collection, University Art Museum, University of New Mexico, Albuquerque

60 Enrique Montenegro (b. 1917), *Woman on a Crosswalk*, 1966 [Tamarind 1510], color lithograph, image 527 x 406 mm (20³/₄ x 16 in), printed by Erwin Erickson. Tamarind Collection, University Art Museum, University of New Mexico, Albuquerque

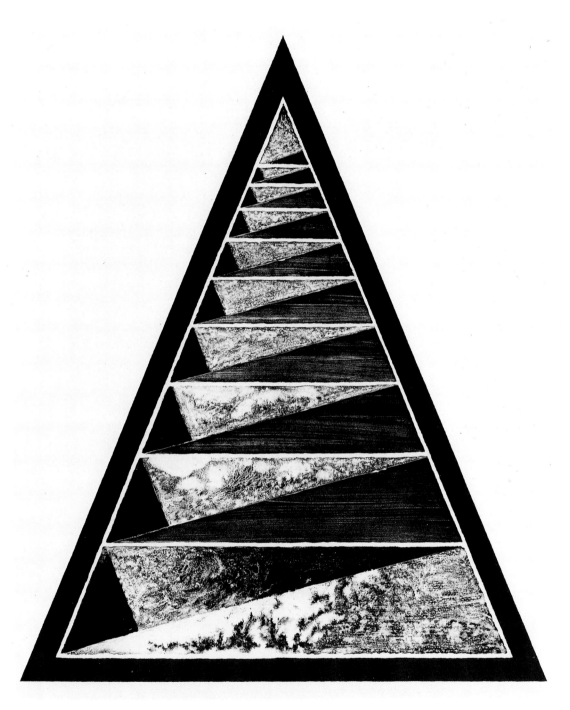

61 Clinton Adams (b. 1918), *Strata*, 1970 [Tamarind 70–101], lithograph,
image and sheet 762 x 559 mm (30 x 22 in), printed by Harry Westlund. Collection,
Museum of Fine Arts, Museum of New Mexico, Santa Fe, purchase with funds donated to
the Museum of New Mexico Foundation [88.199.1]

invitation, and no charge was made for materials or services. In New Mexico it was planned that foundation's support would gradually be withdrawn and that a large part of the printing done for artists would be either on a contractual basis or as a publishing venture, thus to generate funds for continuing support of the institute's programs.[17] We expected that much of our work would be done in collaboration with artists who lived and worked in New Mexico. It was with the thought of bringing these artists to the workshop that, as Tamarind's director, I first spoke with Robert A. Ewing, then curator-in-charge at the Museum of Fine Arts. It was my hope that the museum and Tamarind might cooperate in publication of lithographs by New Mexico artists. Fritz Scholder's name was the first to be mentioned.[18]

Scholder had come to Santa Fe in 1964 (after study in California and Arizona) to teach painting at the Institute of American Indian Arts. As a student, he had worked briefly in lithography but had found the medium "technical" and "laborious." Even so, when Ewing spoke to him of our conversation, Scholder's interest was immediate. Although, as it turned out, the museum was unable to participate, arrangements were soon completed for him to begin work on a suite of lithographs. *Indians Forever*, it would be called.

The important difference that Tamarind made for Scholder—and later for other artists—is clearly revealed by his experience in the making of this suite. He had access to many large stones which could be grained and regrained by the workshop apprentices as he needed them. He could collaborate not with one printer but with several, and in this way his work could go ahead simultaneously at several presses. All materials were on hand; everything was at his fingertips. He could work spontaneously on the stones, while the institute's staff provided the needed technical skills and did the hours of work intrinsic to printmaking. The result was that between December 1970 and March 1971, Scholder completed twenty-one lithographs, eight of which were later chosen for inclusion in *Indians Forever*. During repeated visits to Tamarind throughout the 1970s, he created many memorable images, becoming ever more assured in his command of the medium.

Plate VI

Scholder's immense success may have been a factor in bringing other Native American artists to the workshop. T. C. Cannon, Patrick Swazo Hinds, Dan Namingha, R. C. Gorman, and Jaune Quick-to-See Smith all made prints in the 1970s. Gorman's first lithographs, made in 1971 and 1972, often had a simple directness, as in *Taos Man*. After 1975, Gorman's lithographs were printed by Western Graphics Workshop and Gallery, a firm directed by Ben Q. Adams, a Tamarind-trained master printer. Perhaps in response to the

62

62 R. C. Gorman (b. 1933), *Taos Man*, 1972 [Tamarind 72–265], lithograph,
image and sheet 571 x 463 mm (22^1/$_2$ x 18^1/$_4$ in), printed by Ben Q. Adams. Tamarind
Collection, University Art Museum, University of New Mexico, Albuquerque

63 Jaune Quick-to-See Smith (b. 1940), *Sandhill South*, 1982 [Tamarind 82–314],
color lithograph with handcoloring, image and sheet 762 x 381 mm (30 x 15 in), printed by
Barbara Telleen. Tamarind Collection, University Art Museum, University of New Mexico,
Albuquerque

82

marketplace, Gorman's work became slick and glossy, heavily reliant upon the seductions of blended inking.

Quick-to-See Smith, who came to New Mexico from the Pacific Northwest, combines abstract and representational images in prints that are often narrative in content. Characteristically, as in *Sandhill South*, she achieves rich surfaces through combinations of lithographic printing and hand-coloring.

IN OUR DESIRE TO IDENTIFY publishing projects of importance, we naturally thought of New Mexico's pioneer modernists—Georgia O'Keeffe, Agnes Martin, and Andrew Dasburg—none of whom had been active as printmakers.

O'Keeffe had never made an original print. Aside from John Marin and to a limited extent Marsden Hartley, the artists in the Stieglitz group were not active as printmakers. "Long ago," O'Keeffe said, "when I might have made lithographs, there was no place to do it. Once someone tried to interest me in it. I was given some metal plates—shiny metal plates—but I didn't do anything with them. By the time I could really work at it, it had gone out of my head."[19] Many years later, in November 1963, when there was "a place to do it," Wayne invited O'Keeffe to make lithographs at Tamarind Lithography Workshop in Los Angeles. She was at the workshop, exploring the medium, when President Kennedy was assassinated. Deeply distressed, she interrupted her stay and returned to her home in Abiquiu.

As curator of O'Keeffe's first exhibition in New Mexico, I had come to know her well, and had often visited her in Abiquiu. After Tamarind's move to Albuquerque, I made repeated efforts, beginning in 1970, to engage her interest in making a lithograph, and, at her suggestion, took a fine grey stone to her studio. She loved the smooth, grained surface—I remember her standing by the big north window, running a slender finger along the stone's edge—but she never drew on it. Some years later, disappointed but not surprised, I took the untouched stone back to Tamarind.

Like O'Keeffe, Agnes Martin visited Tamarind but did not make prints there. Martin, who had taught at UNM in the 1950s and now lived in Galisteo, came to Albuquerque in the fall of 1978 to visit her friend Louise Nevelson, who was then undertaking a major project at the workshop. While at Tamarind, Martin watched with interest the activity in the pressroom, but did not respond to a suggestion that she might herself find interest in the medium. Although she made a few serigraphs in the early seventies, printmaking never attracted her full attention.

63

64

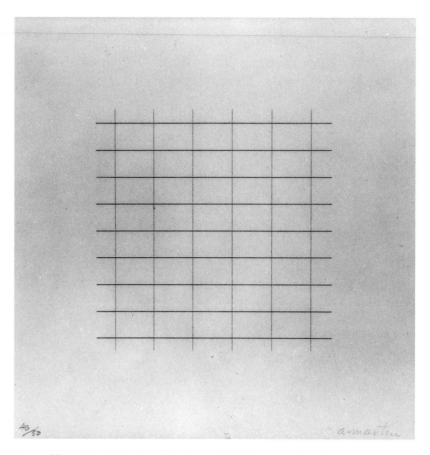

64 Agnes Martin (b. 1912), *On a Clear Day*, 1972–73, color serigraph,
image 171 x 175 mm (6³/₄ x 6⁷/₈ in). Collection, University Art Museum, University of New
Mexico, Albuquerque [75.83]

In the 1960s, Garo Antreasian had invited Andrew Dasburg to make lithographs as a guest artist in connection with the printer-training program, but
Dasburg had been unable to do so. It was not until 1974, when he was eighty-
seven years old, that Dasburg made his first lithographs at Tamarind. Persuaded by his artist friend Earl Stroh and Tamarind's master printer John
Sommers to explore the new medium, Dasburg drew *Ranchos Valley I*. Because
the artist's age made it necessary to limit his trips to Albuquerque, much of
the work was done in his studio at Ranchos de Taos.[20] Dasburg immediately
responded to the flexibility of the process, with particular interest in lithography's ability to accept not only additions but also the subtractions so important to him in his drawings.

65

84

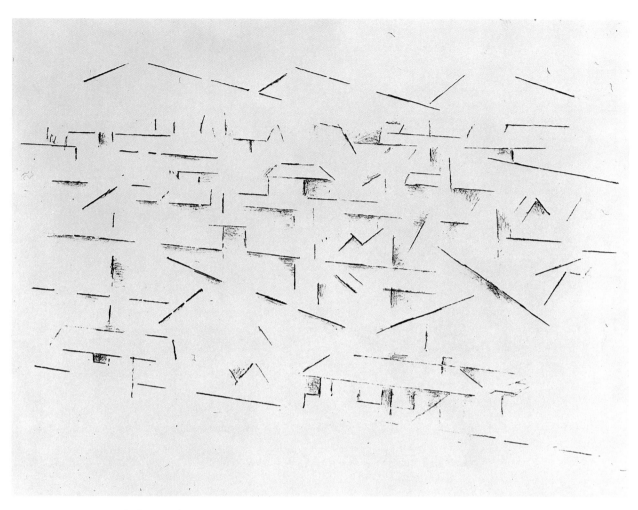

65 Andrew Dasburg (1887–1979), *Ranchos Valley I*, 1974 [Adams 3; Tamarind 74–706], transfer lithograph with tone plate, image and sheet 520 x 628 mm (20¹/₂ x 24¹/₄ in), printed by John Sommers. Tamarind Collection, University Art Museum, University of New Mexico, Albuquerque

66 John Sommers (1927–1987), *Wold (Ambiance)*, 1978 [Tamarind 78–677], color lithograph, image and sheet 460 x 600 mm (18¹/₈ x 23⁵/₈ in), printed by Brynn Jensen. Tamarind Collection, University Art Museum, University of New Mexico, Albuquerque

Following completion of *The Taos Series*, a suite of five lithographs made in 1974 and 1975, Dasburg and Sommers collaborated on a complex lithograph in full color, suggested by one in a series of rich pastel drawings which Dasburg had recently completed. Characteristically, Sommers later recalled, Dasburg drew with a flourish. "He always talked about the speed of the line. He would say, 'that line doesn't have enough speed' or 'it needs more speed.' He was careful about subtle shifts in weight, and how the line ended. Very often he would want to scrape the end of a line down to a certain thinness,"[21] a change he could easily make on the stones Sommers transported back and forth from Albuquerque to Taos. In all, Dasburg made fifteen lithographs between 1974 and 1978, each edition printed by Sommers at Tamarind.

86

Sommers was an outstanding collaborator—sensitive, as a printer must be, to every nuance of an artist's (often unstated) desires—a fine teacher, and an accomplished printmaker. In a series of lithographs completed in the late 1970s, collectively titled *Wold*, Sommers made use of images abstracted from natural forms—the detritus of the landscape: images that "concentrate on the decay that nourishes and rejuvenates the woods" and speak to the "contradictory concept that death creates life."[22]

66

Earl Stroh, who moved to Taos in 1947 and studied with Dasburg and Tom Benrimo, later began work in etching at the Atelier Friedlander in Paris. A meticulous and accomplished draftsman, Stroh believes in the essential role of drawing to the creative act. "The real creative printmaking," he has said, "is done by people who are exploring that medium, not just using it as a hand-done reproduction, a repeat of their statements in other mediums."[23] His work at Tamarind underscores the point. Finding the essence of lithography to lie in the juncture of crayon and stone, he began in 1970 to create a series of remarkable works, culminating in his masterful *Taos Makimono Suite* of 1975–76, completed in collaboration with master printer Lynn Baker. Continuing to work at Tamarind at intervals during the 1980s, Stroh has achieved unprecedented subtleties of color and tone in other lithographs, in which he has continued to explore the vastnesses and complexities of the New Mexico landscape which has been for so long his theme.

67

Plate VII

Another fine draftsman, the *trompe-l'oeil* painter Paul Sarkisian, made lithographs at Tamarind 1971, but was less successful than Stroh, principally because of over-reliance on photographic techniques. Sarkisian wanted his prints to be a pendant to a very large black-and-white painting that he had recently completed. Failing to establish an identity separate from the painting, Sarkisian's Tamarind lithographs remained less than a full realization of his potential as a printmaker.

IT IS IN THE NATURE of a collaborative workshop that its staff of printers must be capable of working successfully with a diversity of artists who make use of a wide range of techniques and processes. At Tamarind, this is essential, as printer fellows in training must learn to respond to a great variety of demands upon their skills and knowledge. Scholder's expressionistic verve, Dasburg's structured precision, Stroh's nuanced tones, and Sarkisian's appropriations from his paintings are but four examples.

More than two hundred artists made lithographs at Tamarind during the 1970s. Some stayed for weeks, during which they completed a large body of

67 Earl Stroh (b. 1924), *Mesa Verde*, ca. 1955, etching, image 276 x 241 mm
(10^7/$_8$ x 9^1/$_2$ in), printed by Leblanc, Paris. Collection, Museum of Fine Arts, Museum of
New Mexico, Santa Fe, gift of Mr. and Mrs. Ford D. Good [2092]

68 Gordon Snidow (b. 1936), *The Baby Sitter*, 1975 [Tamarind 75–155], color lithograph, image 407 x 629 mm (16 x 24³/₄ in), printed by Harry Westlund. Tamarind Collection, University Art Museum, University of New Mexico, Albuquerque

work; others made but one print. Some came from far distant places; others lived in New Mexico. Some were artists of national reputation (among them, Elaine de Kooning, David Hare, Joseph Raffael, Deborah Remington, Louise Nevelson, Ed Ruscha, and Jack Tworkov); others were young artists, not yet established in the field.

No group was more diverse than the New Mexicans. As a matter of principle—and as a practical necessity in the training of printers—Tamarind had always sought work that encompassed a wide range of technical and stylistic directions. New Mexican artists provided this in full measure, from the down-home realism of cowboy artist Gordon Snidow, to the painterly richness of Paul Pletka, the expressionistic exuberance of Sam Scott, and the delicate

68

69, 70

89

69 Paul Pletka (b. 1946), *Raven*, 1979 [Tamarind 79–653], color lithograph,
image and sheet 76.2 x 112 cm (30 x 44 in), printed by Stephen Britko. Tamarind
Collection, University Art Museum, University of New Mexico, Albuquerque

71   fantasies of Michele Bourque Sewards. Clayton Campbell, Harmony Hammond, Frederick Hammersley, Douglas Johnson, Janet Lippincott, Bruce Lowney, Holly Roberts, and Nancy Steen were among the many others who made
lithographs at Tamarind in the seventies.

Also among the New Mexicans were members of the university faculty.
72   Leonard Lehrer, who was chairman of the art department from 1970 to 1974,
worked at Tamarind repeatedly during those years, creating a series of lithographs in which he used the difficult tusche-wash technique with unparalleled
73   control and sensitivity. Betty Hahn and Thomas Barrow, leading figures in the
university's distinguished photography program, combined camera-generated
images with hand-drawn elements, thus bringing into being images that hover

90

70 Sam Scott (b. 1940), *Edge of Autumn*, 1977 [Tamarind 77–137], color lithograph, image and sheet 570 x 766 mm (22 x 30 in), printed by Toby Michel. Tamarind Collection, University Art Museum, University of New Mexico, Albuquerque

between reality and abstraction. Other fine prints were made by Nick Abdalla, Jane Abrams, Robert M. Ellis, Elen Feinberg, Charles Mattox, Sam Smith, John Wenger, and Harry Nadler.

74

75

76

Nadler's *Labyrinth* series again underlines the value of a workshop such as Tamarind, where, because printers and their apprentices perform much of the labor, artists are free to investigate creative possibilities that might otherwise be inaccessible to them. "For me," Nadler says, "the excitement of printmaking is in the proofing. The idea of making large numbers of the same image does not interest me. I make prints in the same spirit I approach my drawing: to see the image change as it is exposed to my intuitive sense of process."[24]

91

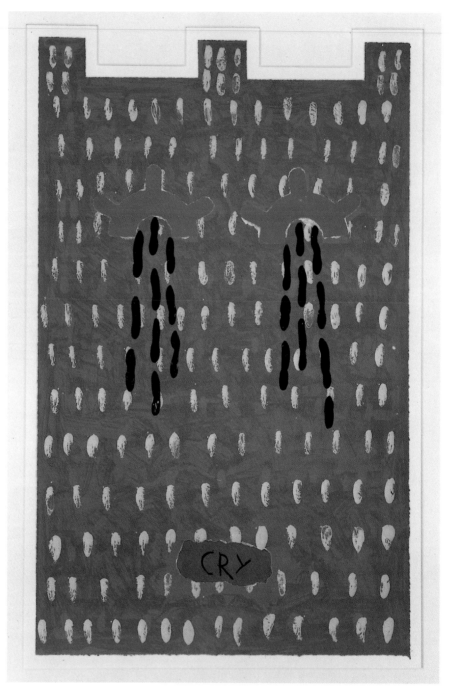

71 Harmony Hammond (b. 1944), *Blue Spirit*, 1978 [Tamarind 78–138], color lithograph, image and sheet 600 x 380 (23⅝ x 15 in), printed by Bill Lagattuta. Tamarind Collection, University Art Museum, University of New Mexico, Albuquerque

72 Leonard Lehrer (b. 1935), *Tepotzotlan*, 1973 [Tamarind 73–670], lithograph,
image and sheet 762 x 559 mm (30 x 22 in), printed by Harry Westlund. Tamarind
Collection, University Art Museum, University of New Mexico, Albuquerque

73 Betty Hahn (b. 1940), *Botanical Layout: Peony,* 1979 [Tamarind 79–630],
color lithograph, image and sheet 610 x 510 mm (24 x 20 in),
printed by Jeffrey Sippel. Tamarind Collection, University Art Museum,
University of New Mexico, Albuquerque

74 Nick Abdalla (b. 1939), *Nude in Red Kimono*, 1979 [Tamarind 79–658],
color lithograph, image and sheet 565 x 765 mm (22¹/₄ x 30¹/₈ in),
printed by Stephen Britko. Tamarind Collection, University Art Museum,
University of New Mexico, Albuquerque

75 Robert M. Ellis (b. 1922), *Rio Grande Gorge #16*, 1982–83 [Tamarind 82–317],
color lithograph, sheet 560 x 764 mm (22 x 30 in), printed by Catherine Kirsch Kuhn.
Tamarind Collection, University Art Museum, University of New Mexico, Albuquerque

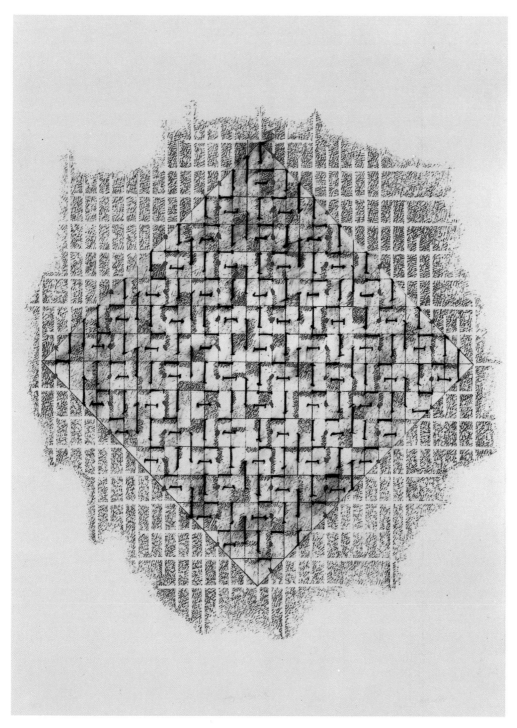

76 Harry Nadler (1930–1990), *Grey Labyrinth*, 1976 [Tamarind 76–623b], color lithograph, sheet 101.6 x 73.7 cm (40 x 29 in), printed by Glenn Brill. Tamarind Collection, University Art Museum, University of New Mexico, Albuquerque

77 Philip Pearlstein (b. 1924), *Ruins at Gran Quivira*, 1975 [Tamarind 75–624], lithograph, image and sheet 485 x 755 mm (19 x 29^1/$_2$ in), printed by Stephen Britko and Russell Hamilton. Tamarind Collection, University Art Museum, University of New Mexico, Albuquerque

Other artists came to Tamarind from New York, California, and elsewhere; some were little affected by the local environment, but others found images here. Philip Pearlstein took advantage of a warm spring day to visit Gran Quivira, where he made a drawing of the ruins directly on a plate. Nathan Oliveira's five prints, each titled *Acoma Hawk*, do not depict a place, but instead evoke its spirit; so, in a different way, does George McNeil's landscape, *Acoma Mesa I*. Paul Brach's *Sandia* recalls the artist's "dreamspace": a misty and romantic world where memories of the distant summers reinforce new perceptions.

Several of the artists who came from California chose to stay in New Mexico. Judy Chicago, who made a suite of color lithographs, *Through the Flower*, at Tamarind in the summer of 1972, later moved to Santa Fe. The Los Angeles painter and ceramist Kenneth Price, who had first worked at Tamarind in Los

77
78

79
80

98

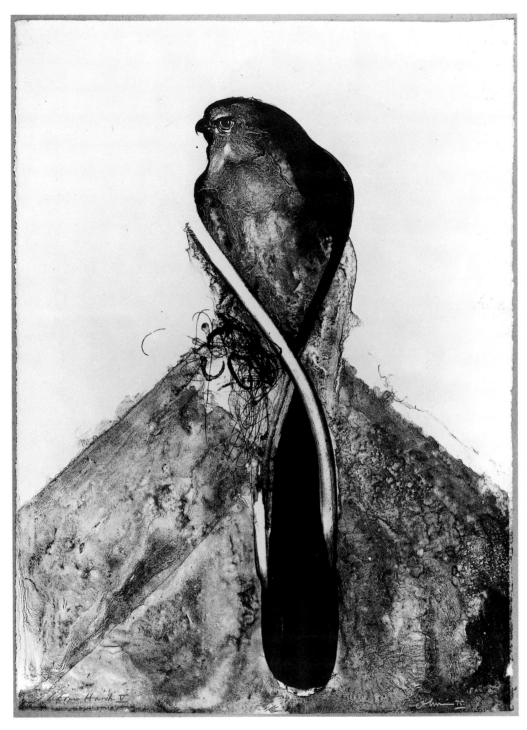

78 Nathan Oliveira (b. 1928), *Acoma Hawk V*, 1975 [Tamarind 75–160a], lithograph, image and sheet 559 x 762 mm (22 x 30 in), printed by Ben Q. Adams and Glenn Brill. Tamarind Collection, University Art Museum, University of New Mexico, Albuquerque

79 George McNeil (b. 1908), *Acoma Mesa I*, 1976 [Tamarind 76–124], color lithograph, image and sheet 559 x 762 mm (22 x 30 in), printed by William Masi. Tamarind Collection, University Art Museum, University of New Mexico, Albuquerque

Plate VIII

Angeles, came to the Albuquerque workshop from his new home in Taos. Price's lithographs became a part of *Tamarind Suite Fifteen*, published in celebration of Tamarind's fifteenth anniversary in 1975.

ARTISTS' LITHOGRAPHY is a complex process that depends heavily upon suppliers and technicians. By 1960, when Tamarind started, many of the companies that had once provided equipment and supporting services were now out of business; Tamarind thus had no choice but to develop new sources. Presses had to be repaired; specialized equipment that was no longer manufactured had to be built by hand.

In Albuquerque, Antreasian came to depend upon Dave Takach, then the

100

80 Paul Brach (b. 1924), *Sandia*, 1980 [Tamarind 80–627], color lithograph,
image and sheet 610 x 758 mm (24 x 29³/₄ in), printed by Yasuotoshi Ishibashi. Tamarind
Collection, University Art Museum, University of New Mexico, Albuquerque

senior engineering technician in UNM's department of mechanical engineering. Takach repaired equipment in the art department workshop, and in the 1960s undertook several assignments for TLW in Los Angeles. After 1970, his presence became increasingly important to Tamarind Institute. Antreasian and Sommers were convinced that a better press could be designed than those then on the market, and in 1974 Takach undertook to build two prototype presses for Sommers and Ben Q. Adams. Later, he formed a company in partnership with Duane R. Garfield and began the commercial manufacture of lithography and intaglio presses, and a wide variety of press equipment. Tamarind's presence in New Mexico thus stimulated not only artists' printmaking but an entire system of support services. The Takach-Garfield Company, still located in Albuquerque, is now one of the United States' principal suppliers of presses and related equipment to shops not only in New Mexico, but in every part of the world.

IX Bruce Lowney (b. 1937), *Gateway*, 1975, color lithograph, image 483 x 660 mm
(19 x 26 in), printed by Robert Arber at Hand Graphics, Ltd., Santa Fe. Collection,
Museum of Fine Arts, Museum of New Mexico, Santa Fe,
gift of John B. Metzenberg [3631]

X Paul Sarkisian (b. 1928), *Envelope (Red Background)*, 1978, color lithograph, image 559 x 533 mm (22 x 21 in), printed by Robert Arber.
Courtesy of Arber and Son Editions, Albuquerque

XI Ron Adams (b. 1934), *Profile in Blue*, 1987, color lithograph, image and sheet
129.5 x 94 cm (51 x 37 in), printed by the artist and David Panosh at Hand Graphics,
Ltd., Santa Fe. Collection, Museum of Fine Arts, Museum of New Mexico, Santa Fe,
purchase prize from "New Mexico '87" with funds donated by Frank Ribelin, Santa Fe
Gallery Association, and Ovenwest Corporation [87.463.1]

XII Judy Chicago (b. 1939), *The Creation*, 1985 [Unified Arts JC.85.4],
color serigraph, image 610 x 889 mm (24 x 35 in), printed by Jim Kraft.
Courtesy of Unified Arts, Albuquerque

XIII Garo Antreasian (b. 1922), *Bebek II*, 1984 [Unified Arts GZA 84.2], color serigraph and pochoir, image 311 x 311 mm (12$^{1}/_{4}$ x 12$^{1}/_{4}$ in), printed by Jim Kraft at Unified Arts, Albuquerque. Courtesy of the artist

XIV Jay Phillips (1954–87), *Descent of Discord*, 1984 [Tamarind 84-323], color lithograph, folded, sheet 688 x 695 mm (27 x 27³/₈ in), printed by Lynne Allen. Tamarind Collection, University Art Museum, University of New Mexico, Albuquerque

XV Thomas Barrow (b. 1938), *Task Mask*, 1989 [21 Steps 89-2], color planograph,
sheet 570 x 455 mm (22^1/$_2$ x 18 in), printed by Jeffrey Ryan at 21 Steps, Albuquerque.
Courtesy of the artist

XVI Frederick Hammersley (b. 1919), *Clout*, 1988 [Tamarind 88-315], color lithograph, image 191 x 191 mm (7^1/$_2$ x 7^1/$_2$ in), printed by Maria Schleiner. Tamarind Collection, University Art Museum, University of New Mexico, Albuquerque

THE CONTEMPORARY SCENE

Gᴀʀᴏ ANTREASIAN served as Tamarind Institute's technical director for two years before resigning in 1972 to devote additional time to the instructional program in lithography which he had developed at UNM. Since coming west from Indiana, he had also found his personal voice in the medium.

Antreasian's earlier work had reflected a wide range of stylistic influences, from social realism in 1942, through various aspects of the School of Paris in the 1950s, to Abstract Expressionism in the early 1960s. When a retrospective exhibition of his prints was held at the Albuquerque Museum in 1988, James Moore noted the changed character of Antreasian's lithographs in the late sixties and early seventies. Gone was the Bonnard-like broken touch and glowing color of such lithographs as *Plums* (1954); the new prints, Moore wrote, are "classically ordered in conception . . . hard-edged, detached, cool, and technically compelling in their precision and formal control."[1] Many reveal Antreasian's fascination with process. In his *Quantum* suite (1966) he began an extended exploration of the permutations possible through use of the blended-inking process,[2] thus creating a series of memorable images; six years later, this provocative, intellectual game reached its apogee in *Untitled T72–121*, a lithographic tour de force in which an unparalleled number of colors were printed simultaneously from a single plate.

It was markedly unusual for a university printmaking program to concentrate upon lithography to the exclusion of relief and intaglio. The rationale at UNM lay partially in the link to Tamarind, but even more in a lack of space for expansion. Lithography could survive (barely) in a small basement studio, but

81

82

81 Garo Antreasian (b. 1922), *Plums*, 1954, color lithograph, sheet 451 x 350 mm
(17³/₄ x 13³/₄ in), printed by the artist. Courtesy of the artist

etching—with its inevitable acid fumes—could not safely be accommodated there. When Jane Abrams joined the faculty in 1971, it had been thought that a new art building would soon provide a studio for intaglio printmaking, but unexpected delays in construction were to cause a five-year wait before a full range of printmaking courses could be offered.

Abrams was not similarly delayed in her own work. The sophisticated execution and playful wit of her color intaglio prints from the seventies and early eighties brought her national recognition. Ironically, after the long wait, the university's newly completed intaglio studio fell short of expectations, and at the top of Abrams's career as a printmaker, she suffered adverse effects

82 Garo Antreasian (b. 1922), *Untitled 72–121*, 1972 [Tamarind 72–121], color lithograph,
image 584 x 902 mm (23 x 35$\frac{1}{2}$ in), printed by Christopher Cordes. Tamarind Collection,
University Art Museum, University of New Mexico, Albuquerque

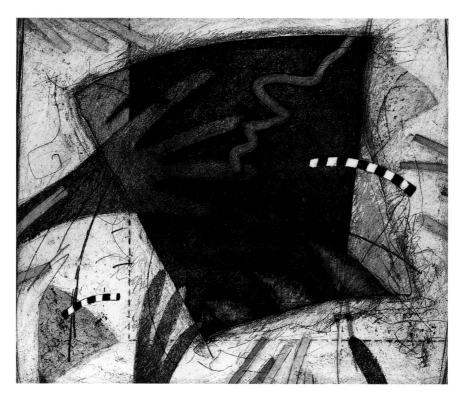

83 Jane Abrams (b. 1940), *Fumbling at the Speed of Light*, 1983, color intaglio, image 375 x 457 mm (14³/₄ x 18 in), printed by the artist. Courtesy of the artist

from chemicals used in the intaglio process. Unable to continue her work in printmaking, Abrams turned to painting and, while artist-in-residence at the Roswell Museum and Art Center in 1985 and 1986, created a series of large, expressionist landscapes that proclaimed a total shift in direction.

In 1987, following quickly on Jane Abrams's decision to abandon print-making, the continuity of the UNM printmaking program was further disrupted by Garo Antreasian's retirement from teaching and, a few months later, by John Sommers's sudden death. Following a period of transition, the program assumed a new direction in 1990 under the guidance of Lydia Madrid and José Rodriguez. While their work differs substantially in style, both artists are strongly affected by personal family histories and Hispanic cultural traditions. Rodriguez, who works with assurance in several print media, is at *84* his best in such strongly felt prints as *Sagrado Corazon*, an archetypal portrait of haunting intensity.

106

84 José Rodriguez (b. 1959). *Sagrado Corazon*, 1988, etching and drypoint,
image 703 x 498 mm (27⅝ x 19⅝ in), printed by the artist. Courtesy of University Art
Museum, University of New Mexico, Albuquerque

At New Mexico State University in Las Cruces, the visual arts were slow to develop within a context that emphasized agriculture and engineering. Instruction in printmaking did not move forward until 1978, when it was stimulated by the appointment of Spencer Fidler, an intaglio printmaker who had studied with Lasansky at Iowa. An effective teacher and an accomplished artist, Fidler created a lively environment at NMSU, but without substantial effect upon printmaking in southern New Mexico. Although his students won awards and grants while in Las Cruces, they typically went elsewhere to work. It is, he sadly comments, a "sorry statement for us in the south."[3]

The instruction Abrams and Fidler offered at the universities was very much within the mainstream of the American intaglio tradition. By contrast, the program developed earlier by Seymour Tubis at the Institute of American Indian Arts (IAIA) in Santa Fe had reflected the unique character of that institution. Established in 1962 by the Bureau of Indian Affairs (United States Department of the Interior) to provide advanced instruction in the visual arts to Native American students, the school soon attracted talented young artists from all parts of the United States. Although experienced in all of the principal printmaking media, Tubis sought to avoid unnecessary technical complexities and to make his students aware of alternative possibilities: "Materials such as slate, leather, sand, feathers, cloth, and bark, with which they already had a familiarity, could be just as valid as the traditional printmaking tools, supplies, and surfaces."[4] During Tubis's eighteen years at IAIA, his prints—including *Pueblo Ceremonial Trio*, which he cut simply and directly into a coarse-grained plank—were affected both by this attitude and by the influence of Native American art forms.

The intaglio media, however, became the "major source of expression" for the students at IAIA. These media, Tubis writes, "allowed experimentation, reflection on their roots and personal idioms, as well as the gratification of mastering a craft which, in many ways, became allied to some of their traditional crafts."[5] During the high point of the IAIA's printmaking program, fine intaglio prints were made by such students as Benjamin Buffalo, Grey Cohoe, Benjamin Harjo, Jr., Brenda Holden, Courtney Moyah, Wenceslaus D. Riley, and Mike Romero. Although Tubis left the school in 1981, printmaking classes continue under the direction of Jean LaMarr.

In Roswell, the Artist-in-Residence program begun in 1967 by the Roswell Museum and Art Center (with primary support from Donald B. Anderson), provided an important resource for artists from all parts of the United States, some of substantial reputation, others young and unknown. Howard Cook, the

85

86

87

85 Spencer Fidler (b. 1944), *Madness*, 1989, color intaglio, image 914 x 610 mm
(36 x 24 in), printed by the artist. Courtesy of the artist

86 Seymour Tubis (b. 1919), *Pueblo Ceremonial Trio*, 1975, woodcut,
image 441 x 610 mm (17³/₈ x 24 in), printed by the artist. Courtesy of the artist

87 Mike Romero (b. 1950), *Mirror of Life Past*, 1973, etching, image 318 x 381 mm
(12¹/₂ x 15 in), printed by the artist. Courtesy of Seymour Tubis

first to receive a grant within this program, went there as a painter (he made
only two prints after 1955); Elmer Schooley also went as a painter and, at
the conclusion of his grant, decided to remain and work in Roswell. In the
twenty-three years between 1967 and 1990, sixteen grants were given to
printmakers, including, from New Mexico, Jane Abrams, Mary Ahern, Bruce
Lowney (who received two grants), Frank McCulloch, and Michele Bourque
Sewards. For the artists who received them, these uniquely structured residencies—necessarily limited in number—provided an opportunity to work in
"an idyllic environment. . . . For me," Sewards said, "Roswell was a magical,
peaceful place where worries were at a minimum and life was full of stimulation
because of the energy generated by other artists there."[6] Most welcome was
the freedom "from schedules and the stupor they induce," two artists wrote,

88
89

111

88 Frank McCulloch (b. 1930), *79.5*, 1979, color lithograph, image 597 x 410 mm
(23^1/$_2$ x 16^1/$_8$ in), printed by the artist. Courtesy of the artist

112

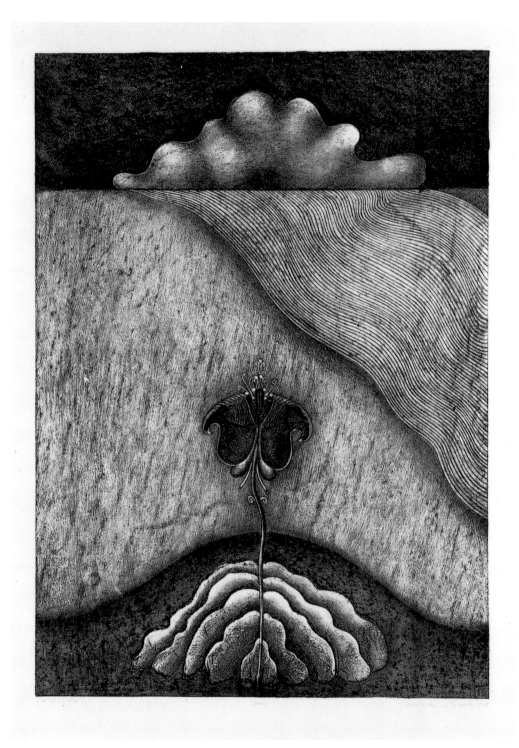

89 Michele Bourque Sewards (b. 1944), *Rain*, 1974, lithograph, image 543 x 393 mm
(21¼ x 15⅜ in), printed by the artist. Courtesy of the artist

"[we] stayed year-long in that place between consciousness and sleep where creative leaps are born."[7] Such freedom from schedules was of particular importance to McCulloch, for whom the Roswell grant provided a welcome interruption in his work as a teacher of art (including printmaking) at Albuquerque's Highland High School.[8] For all of the printmakers, the Roswell residencies provided not only a "gift of time" but also access to a fully equipped printmaking studio, unlimited supplies, and—equally important—freedom from distractions.

IT WAS MY HOPE, when Tamarind Institute was established as a division of the UNM College of Fine Arts, that the proximity of the institute and the department of art might serve to counteract what I perceived (and still perceive) to be the dangers of specialization. Because most of the world's fine prints have been made by painters, not by specialist-printmakers, it seems to me wrongheaded that in American art schools and universities young artists are encouraged (and often required) to specialize. Students of painting, sculpture, or photography seldom have an opportunity to make prints unless they are willing to enroll in technical printmaking courses. The situation *in* the schools is thus very unlike the situation *outside* the schools, where a high percentage of the more significant prints are made in collaborative workshops.

Earlier on, in the 1930s and 1940s, lithography had been taught differently at some American art schools—notably at the Art Students League in New York and the Colorado Springs Fine Arts Center—where students were not obliged to learn the technical processes of printing unless they chose to do so.[9] The printer-training program at Tamarind provided an ideal opportunity to establish a similar structure. Beginning in the mid-1970s we invited graduate students in painting, sculpture, and photography to participate in a new program of collaborative printmaking; I gave critiques—later taken over by John Sommers—and the students' work was printed by the institute's printer fellows. The fine work done by the gifted young artists who participated in this program conclusively demonstrated the value of the concept.

IN LOS ANGELES, one of Tamarind's first objectives (as set forth in Wayne's proposal to the Ford Foundation) had been to "create a pool of master artisan-printers in the United States," and to encourage these printers to open new lithographic workshops in cities across the nation. The effect of these workshops, which rapidly grew in number, was both to stimulate an interest in

114

printmaking among American artists and—by creating opportunities for apprentices—to create a "second generation" of printers, beyond those trained at Tamarind. Among the workshops established in the early sixties, one of the most successful—first called Gemini, Ltd., and later Gemini G.E.L. (Graphics Editions Limited)—was begun in 1965 by Tamarind printers Bernard Bleha and Kenneth Tyler.[10] As assistants, they recruited students from Southern California's art schools and universities, among them Ron Adams, who between 1968 and 1973 worked with Tyler on collaborative projects with such artists as Sam Francis, Jasper Johns, and Robert Rauschenberg.

In 1973, when Tyler left Gemini, Adams also left. He wanted to establish a workshop of his own, and his wife Hazel Jaramillo, a native New Mexican, persuaded him to consider New Mexico: "I also realized," Adams later said, "that apart from Tamarind Institute in Albuquerque, there wasn't another lithography press between Denver and Phoenix. I knew that artists from all over the region would be interested in working in a centrally located place like Santa Fe."[11] Adams and Jaramillo formed a partnership, leased a warehouse building adjacent to Santa Fe's old railroad yards—not then surrounded by fashionable restaurants and boutiques—and moved forward to found Hand Graphics, Ltd., the first private-enterprise, lithography workshop to be established in New Mexico. Late in 1973, Robert Arber, who had been a printer fellow at Tamarind, joined the partnership. When remodelling was completed, they began to work with artists, among them Bruce Lowney, whose enigmatic *Gateway* was printed by Arber in collaboration with the artist. Because Arber subsequently found burdensome the strain of commuting to Santa Fe from Alameda (a village in Albuquerque's north valley, where he had his own press and was already doing some printing),[12] he withdrew from the partnership to establish his own shop, later named Arber and Son Editions.

Plate IX

Gradually improving his press room and adding new equipment, Arber collaborated with Paul Sarkisian, Bruce Nauman, and Carl Johansen to produce a diversity of exciting prints. The convincing super-reality of Sarkisian's *Envelope* achieves a miraculous intensity; Nauman's cryptic *Earth-World* avoids banality through the visual richness of its execution; while Johansen's *Artist and Model* depicts the artist confronted by his private vision of a world haunted by angels, demons, and the history of art.

Plate X

90

91

In Santa Fe, Ron Adams continued with Hand Graphics until 1987, when he sold the workshop to printer Michael Costello. Trained as an artist in Los Angeles before beginning work at Gemini, Adams had for more than fifteen

90 Bruce Nauman (b. 1941), *Earth-World*, 1986, lithograph, image and sheet 76.2 x 111.8 cm (30 x 44 in), printed by Robert Arber, Arber and Son Editions, Albuquerque. Collection, University Art Museum, University of New Mexico, Albuquerque, purchase, Julius Rolshoven Memorial Fund [86.199]

91 Carl H. Johansen (b. 1946), *Artist and Model*, 1975, color lithograph,
image 559 x 737 mm (22 x 29 in), printed by Robert Arber. Courtesy of Arber and Son
Editions, Albuquerque

Plate XI

years subordinated his own work to printing. Now he celebrated his independence in a masterful color lithograph, *Profile in Blue*, a self-portrait as printer. He sits with quiet dignity and strength on his Brand press, roller in hand at day's end, light streaming through the window behind his shoulders.

Costello had been in the field for seven years before joining Adams at Hand Graphics in 1982. With the assistance of Robert Brady and Eric Lindgren, he collaborates principally with artists in the Santa Fe area, where his multipress workshop provides the high professional skills that are essential to the making of complex color lithographs and intaglio prints. A pleasant gallery provides space for exhibition of completed editions, many of which are published by the workshop.

Among the artists who have worked collaboratively at Hand Graphics (either with Adams or Costello) are Woody Gwyn, Zara Kriegstein, Sergio Moyano, Dolona Roberts, and Paul Shapiro. Their varied works are sufficient to establish that there is no "shop style." Gwyn has found a fresh vision of the western landscape at a time when, Mark Stevens observes, "our eyes have become sticky from looking at the schlock produced by artists of the purple mountain majesty school."[13] In *Interstate*, Gwyn achieves a mysterious tension between the New Mexican landscape and the highway that bisects it; they are "two solitudes that protect and touch and greet each other."[14] Moyano, by contrast, uses lithography's autographic and gestural directness to create the exuberant black-and-white image *Backstage (SFO)*. Shapiro chooses intaglio rather than lithography for his ominous triptych *The Golem*, and, through use of a complex combination of plate-making techniques, achieves a richness of surface that contributes greatly to the expressive power of his image.

A very different physical environment is provided at Stephen Britko's Naravisa Press, located in the juniper-studded hills near the village of Cerrillos. After founding two shops in Illinois, Britko had served for two years as Tamarind's master printer and studio manager before opening Naravisa, first in Albuquerque, then at his new location in the country, where he built a traditional New Mexico home and a separate building to house his studio and a small apartment for use by visiting artists. Having spent hectic years at other shops, it was (and is) Britko's intention to work with one artist at a time. Luis Jimenez, Steve Forbis, Russell Hamilton, Steve Hanks, and Tom Palmore are among those who have worked at Naravisa.

Jimenez achieved national recognition in the 1970s for his pop sculptures, in many of which he explores the myths of the Old West; since then he has made lithographs in several of the workshops, most recently at Naravisa,

118

92 Woody Gwyn (b. 1944), *Interstate*, 1981 [Hand Graphics 81–128–L], color lithograph, image 508 x 457 mm (20 x 18 in), printed by Eric Lindgren. Courtesy of Hand Graphics, Ltd., Santa Fe

119

93 Sergio Moyano (b. 1934), *Backstage (SFO)*, 1988, lithograph, image 518 x 489 mm
(20³/₈ x 19¹/₄ in), printed by Michael Costello. Courtesy of Hand Graphics, Ltd., Santa Fe

120

94 Paul Shapiro (b. 1939), *The Golem*, 1988 [Hand Graphics 87–580–E],
photo-etching with aquatint, roulette, drypoint, motor tool, and open-bite manipulation;
three images, each 457 x 556 mm (18 x 21⁷/₈ in), printed by Michael Costello.
Courtesy of Hand Graphics, Ltd., Santa Fe

95 Luis Jimenez (b. 1940), *Snake and Eagle*, 1985 [Naravisa LJ 88–15], color lithograph, image and sheet 584 x 775 mm (23 x 30½ in), printed by Stephen Britko, commissioned by the Museum of Fine Arts, Museum of New Mexico, Santa Fe, for benefit sale, with support from the Adair Margo Gallery, El Paso, and Frank Ribelin [89.424.01]

96 Steve Forbis (b. 1950), *Sharing Traditions*, 1982 [Naravisa SF 82–27], lithograph, image 156 x 225 mm (6¹/₈ x 8⁷/₈ in), printed by Stephen Britko. Courtesy of Naravisa Press

where his freshly drawn *Snake and Eagle* was printed as a commission from the Museum of Fine Arts. Forbis, a meticulous draftsman who has a background in anthropology, continues in the path of earlier artists who sought to create accurate visual documents of life in the Pueblos of the Rio Grande Valley.

95
96

In Albuquerque, Western Graphics Workshop is known primarily as publisher of the color lithographs made by R. C. Gorman. Its director, the artist and master printer Ben Q. Adams, also publishes his own work and that of Nancy Steen, an experienced artist who has made prints at several New Mexico workshops, including Tamarind Institute and Hand Graphics, Ltd.

ALL OF THE PRINT PROCESSES benefited from the collaborative environment that Tamarind introduced into New Mexico. While a number of the workshops continued to specialize in lithography, it soon became possible for an artist to work in any print medium.

Robert Blanchard, a printer expert in both intaglio and lithography (he had been a printer fellow at Tamarind), opened the Custom Etching Studio in Albuquerque in 1980. Three years later he expanded his small workshop and

123

shared space with Cuervo Creative Papers, directed by artist-printer Russell Hamilton.[15] Blanchard has undertaken a number of collaborative projects, the most ambitious of which is a suite of color aquatints made by Santa Fe artist Harold Joe Waldrum. The suite *Las Sombras de Los Edificios Religiosos de Nuevo México Norte*, printed on handmade Cuervo paper, took two years to complete. Whatever the merit of Waldrum's images (they were praised by William Peterson),[16] there can be no question but that the artist and printer took "the aquatint medium through a range of effects, from luxurious, velvet darks to delicate granular washes as light as a butterfly's wing."[17] More recently, Waldrum and Blanchard have collaborated on a series of color linoleum cuts, using the reductive method developed by Picasso in 1959.[18]

New Mexico's premier screen-printing studio is Unified Arts in Albuquerque, located in a spacious south valley compound that includes a beautifully restored adobe house, an apartment for visiting artists, and a modern, well-equipped workshop. Founded in 1972 by Jim Kraft (who later was joined by Judy Booth, formerly assistant director of Tamarind Institute), Unified Arts has sought to work with artists who want to make "exceptional" serigraphs. Able to handle work of large scale and great complexity, Kraft and Booth welcome "the challenge of an artist who wants to push the medium."[19] That interest has been evident in many of their projects, increasingly so in the 1980s. New Mexican artists who have worked at Unified Arts include Judy Chicago, Tom Palmore, Garo Antreasian, Beverly Magennis, and Joel Peter Witkin.

A second screen-printing workshop, Serigraphics, also located in Albuquerque, was established in 1976 by Harry Westlund, who had been for three years printer-in-charge of Tamarind's contract printing and publishing workshop. Though the artists who worked with Westlund were, for the most part, less prominent than those who worked at Unified Arts, the existence of a second workshop gave further impetus to serigraphy in New Mexico.[20]

Among the many artists attracted to the medium by its newly expanded potential was Judy Chicago, who undertook a series of large-scale prints at Unified Arts—a series that culminated in *The Creation*. As shimmering colors emerge from the black void of the paper, they become a metaphor for her conception of the radiant explosion through which the earth gave birth to life. As in all fine works, the complex technical means (forty-five colors were printed from nine screens) are at the service of the image; they do not overwhelm it. Again, in Tom Palmore's *Rare Southwestern Toucan* the "great and earnest labor" of the artist and his printers has been made invisible.[21] We see

Plate VII

97

124

97 Tom Palmore (b. 1945), *Rare Southwestern Toucan*, 1980, combined color serigraph and lithograph, image 864 x 635 mm (34 x 25 in), printed by Jim Kraft and Stephen McClelland, Unified Arts, Albuquerque; Joseph Petruzzelli and Rod Shopis, Siena Studios, New York. Courtesy of Unified Arts, Albuquerque

98 Beverly Magennis (b. 1942), *Partial Construction of Improbable Sculpture 1*, 1981
[Unified Arts BML.81.1a], color serigraph, constructed in three dimensions,
image 487 x 365 x 19 mm (19³/₁₆ x 14³/₈ x ³/₄ in), printed by Jim Kraft. Courtesy of
Unified Arts, Albuquerque

126

only the delightful toucan, which Palmore has perched incongruously in front of a stereotypical, paint-by-the-numbers, desert landscape.

Artists who move from one print medium to another—or who (like Palmore) combine two media, serigraphy and lithography, in a single image—frequently find that the technical challenge leads to discovery of new ways to develop a personal image. So it was with Antreasian, when he made a series of serigraphs at Unified Arts in 1983 and 1984. In *Bebek II* he combined serigraphy with pochoir, using stencils to apply powdered pigment to wet ink, thus achieving transitional shifts of color that resembled (but were different from) those achieved in lithographic blended inking. He also gained new dimensions: "I wanted to work at a larger size than was locally possible in lithography; I wanted an embossment that I could not accomplish on a lithograph press; I wanted a density of ink."[22]

Plate VIII

The physical alteration of the surface of a print through embossment is but a step on the path to a third dimension. Nationally, as well as in New Mexico, artists have sought to give the print a new "presence" by manipulating the paper upon which it rests. At Tamarind in 1973, sculptor Gerald C. Johnson made an untitled suite of lithographs in which minimalist images were created entirely by creasing and folding sheets that had first been printed in a single color. In 1981, working at Unified Arts, Beverly Magennis moved her "constructed serigraph," *Partial Construction of Improbable Sculpture I*, fully into the third dimension. At Tamarind, Jay Phillips made large lithographs of irregular shape, designed to be printed on both sides of the paper. Marjorie Devon wrote of the "refreshing contradictions [that] manifest themselves in these abstracted landscapes: the juxtapositions of lively brushstrokes and hard edge stripes and grids, the three-dimensional fold against the flat sheet and the unexpected use of color."[23] Also at Tamarind, Gail Gash made two series of lithographs which playfully juxtaposed reality and illusion. In *Shin Hanga III* she draws portions of the texture in a manner to fool the eye; others, she cuts, folds, and ties—closing them away from all but imagination. Martie Zelt leaves the conventions of two-dimensional printmaking still further behind in a series of prints made in 1983, each titled *Return to A-qq*, in which she combines paper, printed either by lithography and xerography, with collage and fragments of cloth, sewn together to comprise richly irregular compositions suspended (and supported) by wooden dowels.

98

99

100

Technically the most innovative of the New Mexican print shops is Jeffrey Ryan's 21 Steps (also in Albuquerque), which makes use of a new process best described as planography. Like lithography, this process is planographic

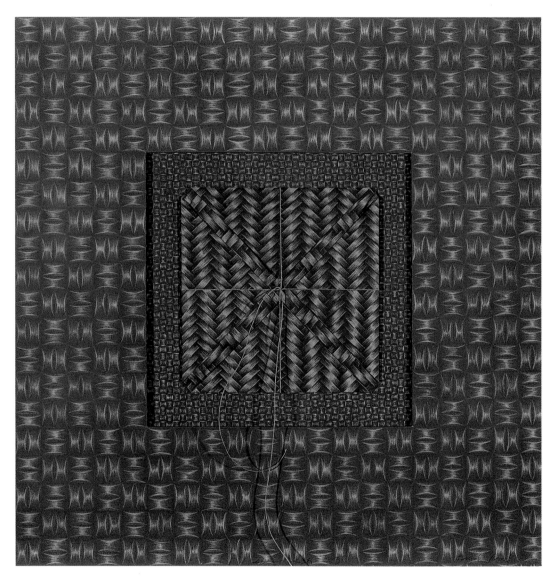

99 Gail Gash (b. 1951), *Shin Hanga III*, 1983 [Tamarind 83–310], color lithograph, folded, with string, image and sheet 510 x 510 mm (20 x 20 in), printed by Barbara Telleen. Tamarind Collection, University Art Museum, University of New Mexico, Albuquerque

128

100 Martie Zelt (b. 1930), *Return to A-qq #3*, 1983 [Tamarind 83–303], color lithograph, sewn, with paper collage and cloth, 535 x 690 mm (21 x 27^1/$_8$ in), printed by Catherine Kirsch Kuhn. Tamarind Collection, University Art Museum, University of New Mexico, Albuquerque (printing done from a flat surface), but unlike lithography, it does not depend upon the mutual repulsion of grease and water (water is not used in printing the plates). The result is an entirely new kind of print with a visual character that differs from that of any other medium. For photographic imagery, Ryan makes use of silicon-coated, light-sensitive plates manufactured in Japan (although the process was invented in America); for hand-drawn elements, he uses other silicon-coated plates (both types of plates may be combined in a print).

The creative possibilities of planography are made evident through comparison of two prints developed in collaboration with Ryan. Though both artists employed photographic processes in creation of their images, the resultant prints differ greatly in character. For *Layered Passages* Vera Henderson Sprunt made use of a photograph of the petroglyphs on eastern Utah's Newspaper Rock; the duotone plates made from the photograph were altered by the artist and combined with hand-drawn elements to create a delicate and subtle composition, shifting in space and time. *Task Mask* by Thomas Barrow underwent even more radical transformations. Using a video camera, Barrow converted a nineteenth-century engraving of a mask from the Sandwich Islands into digital code; then, with the image on a monitor, he used a computergraphics program to make extensive changes in it. Finally, after all but completely transforming the image, he made a color transparency from the monitor. Separations from this transparency were then used to make the plates from which *Task Mask* was printed.

AS THE 1980s CAME TO AN END, collaborative printmaking was well established in New Mexico. Tamarind Institute continues to publish fine lithographs under the leadership of Marjorie Devon (I retired from Tamarind's directorship in 1985). By intention, so as to provide the breadth of experience necessary in the training of student printers, the work undertaken at Tamarind ranges from the unconventional to the traditional: from the prints of photographer Steve Yates (in which hand-drawn elements are superimposed on Ektachrome prints) to the editions of painters Robert Peterson and Tom Berg, drawn with crayon on stone—Bolton Brown's "noble method," the heart and soul of lithography.[24]

In celebration of the University of New Mexico's centennial year in 1989, Tamarind published a suite of prints by fifteen faculty (and former faculty) artists, which included the superb nonfigurative lithographs *Clout* and *Untitled* by Frederick Hammersley and Timothy App, respectively; the softly elegant

101

Plate XV

102

103

104

Plate XVI

105

130

101 Vera Henderson Sprunt (b. 1954), *Layered Passages*, 1990 [21 Steps 90–1],
color planograph, image 230 x 230 mm (9 x 9 in), printed by Jeffrey Ryan at 21 Steps,
Albuquerque. Courtesy of the artist

102 Steve Yates (b. 1949), *Quartet EPC, I,* 1988 [Tamarind 88–304], Ektachrome print with lithographic overprinting, image and sheet 507 x 608 mm (20 x 24 in), printed by the artist and Eileen Foti. Tamarind Collection, University Art Museum, University of New Mexico, Albuquerque

132

103 Robert Peterson (b. 1943), *Shop Towel over Block*, 1983 [Tamarind 83–326],
color lithograph, image and sheet 457 x 610 mm (18 x 24 in), printed by Marcia Brown.
Tamarind Collection, University Art Museum, University of New Mexico, Albuquerque

104 Tom Berg (b. 1943), *Dark Adirondack*, 1988 [Tamarind 88–353], color lithograph, image 346 x 359 mm (13⅝ x 14⅛ in), printed by Eileen Foti. Tamarind Collection, University Art Museum, University of New Mexico, Albuquerque

134

105 Timothy App (b. 1947), *Untitled*, 1988 [Tamarind 88–339], color lithograph,
image 203 x 304 mm (8 x 12 in), printed by Heather Hoover. Tamarind Collection,
University Art Museum, University of New Mexico, Albuquerque

106 Elen Feinberg (b. 1955), *Dawn*, 1988 [Tamarind 88–325], color lithograph,
image 203 x 203 mm (8 x 8 in), printed by Jeffrey Ryan. Tamarind Collection, University
Art Museum, University of New Mexico, Albuquerque

106
107
Dawn by painter Elen Feinberg; and the provocative *Trinitite Tempest* by
photographer Patrick Nagatani. These and other memorable images made the
Centennial Suite a fitting coda to the 1980s.

As if to prove that contemporary prints need not always be "bigger, brighter,
and bolder,"[25] Tamarind undertook in 1990 two additional projects at small
scale: *Seis Santeros*, a portfolio of color lithographs by traditional wood carvers
from northern New Mexico, and *Artists' Impressions*, a suite of small, black-
and-white lithographs by artists from throughout the United States. Among
the lithographs created for *Seis Santeros*, the muted colors and honest grace
of the prints made by Félix López and Luis Tapia most clearly reflect the
enduring vitality of New Mexico's native folk traditions.[26] By contrast, the
prints included in *Artists' Impressions* exhibit the diversity of contemporary
art in America, comprising a wide range of images, from geometric abstraction
to romantic fantasy.[27]

136

"TRINITITE TEMPEST"   T1   NAGATANI

107 Patrick Nagatani (b. 1945), *Trinitite Tempest*, 1988 [Tamarind 88–348],
color lithograph, image 252 x 339 mm (10 x 13³/₈ in), printed by Jeffrey Ryan. Tamarind
Collection, University Art Museum, University of New Mexico, Albuquerque

137

AS THE NINETIES BEGIN, however, serious questions persist with respect to the economic, ethical, and aesthetic future of the fine print: questions which—though not limited to New Mexico—are of particular importance here. On a per capita basis, the number of artists working in this state is the highest in the nation; similarly, the number of collaborative workshops (in actual number, New Mexico ranks third, behind New York and California).

The cost of making prints has risen sharply over the last decade. In large part, this is a result of inflation; a weakened dollar has also added to the price of imported papers. Simultaneously, a sluggish economy has caused a soft market for the prints that artists produce; and the rising overhead faced by art galleries has made them less willing to publish (or even to handle) prints which, when sold, bring them small commissions. Given this economic climate, the collaborative workshops find it necessary to work primarily with artists whose prints can find a quick market; this, in New Mexico, too often means prints that are responsive to the tastes of tourists. The effect is to discourage serious artists whose work is not so oriented.

Artists who make prints opportunistically only add to the problems. Frank McCulloch is concerned that many of the prints made in collaborative workshops are made by "gun-slingers . . . one-shot artists who have no commitment to printmaking."[28] Artists need not be printers—witness Picasso—but they should be sufficiently involved in an interaction with the medium to use it creatively. Many of the one-shot prints are little more than hand-made reproductions of the artists' paintings; that is their reason for being.

Ethics in the field are, at times, no better than the economics. Taking advantage of the fact that in art, as in other fields, the American public is frequently ill informed, shady publishers and print galleries have pursued policies of disinformation. Offset reproductions signed in pencil masquerade as original prints, and are advertised in a manner that skirts the edge of legality. Stephen Britko speaks for many printers when he comments on the cynicism he encounters:

> The thing that most upsets me is when I feel that artists don't care. There is a new breed of artists . . . for whom money is everything. Their attitude has become a real problem; the only thing they can see is the dollar sign. As a printer, that really hurts me—and it hurts their work.
>
> People are spending a lot of money on prints that are nothing more than offset reproductions. Galleries are not educating people to recognize the difference between such reproductions and fine, hand-printed lithographs.[29]

138

The task of educating a discriminating audience for the visual arts is not an easy one. The museums clearly have a critical role—and in printmaking they have not played it as actively as might be wished. In New Mexico we continue to suffer from the provincial attitude with which our major newspapers view the arts. The state's leading art publication, *Artspace* magazine, appears too often to be swayed by its advertisers; it has, in any event, seldom given attention to prints and printmakers.

Thomas Carlyle called history "a distillation of rumor." In the visual arts—paraphrasing Carlyle—we might speak of history as a "distillation of critical judgments," and recognize that as we near the present day a lack of temporal perspective makes the outcome of such distillation increasingly uncertain. We are able to see the prints made by such artists as Baumann, Nordfeldt, Cook, and Yunkers in historical context—a context not yet established for the prints of the 1970s and 1980s. The artists who formed the early art colonies worked within small, geographically contained communities, and—whatever their differences of style or philosophy—they were part of a common culture. The Albuquerque modernists of the 1950s retained a sense of group identity. Thereafter, however, New Mexico was profoundly changed by events, and those who sought to cling to old myths became anachronisms.

Even without Tamarind's move from Los Angeles, these changes would have led to a new kind of printmaking here. With Tamarind in Albuquerque, however, that process was greatly accelerated, and within the space of a very few years printmaking in New Mexico moved from a *retardataire* position to one of national prominence. The subsequent establishment of other collaborative workshops reinforced this fact, with the result that, as we enter the 1990s, New Mexico's artists and printers have an importance in the field that is disproportionate to their numbers. Whatever the economic problems, it is a vital scene with excellent prospects for continuation. "The history of an art," Ezra Pound observed, "is the history of masterwork, not of failures, or mediocrity."[30]

NOTES

CHAPTER 1

1. Goldman, *American Prints*, 34.

2. Prints made by artists in New Mexico are barely mentioned in Eldredge, Schimmel, and Truettner, *Art in New Mexico;* or Udall, *Modernist Painting in New Mexico;* and receive only slightly more attention in Coke, *Taos and Santa Fe.*

3. Pennell, *Lithography and Lithographers*, 246.

4. Peet, *American Women of the Etching Revival*, 12.

5. For the etching revival see Watrous, *Century of American Printmaking*, chap. 1, "Entering the Mainstream of Printmaking."

6. For the Painter-Gravers of America, see Adams, *American Lithographers*, 19; and Field, et al., *American Prints*, 19–22. Most members of such earlier print organizations as the New York Etching Club, the Cincinnati Etching Club, and the Philadelphia Society of Etchers were specialist-printmakers, not painters who made prints.

7. The Taos Society of Artists was organized in July 1915; see White, *Taos Society of Artists*, 5, 23.

8. Eldredge, Schimmel, and Truettner, *Paths to Taos and Santa Fe*, 13.

9. Robertson, *Gerald Cassidy*, n.p.

10. On evidence of correspondence in the clipping files of the New York Public Library, many of Cassidy's early lithographs were printed by the Latham Litho & Printing Company of Long Island City, New York. By 1918 or 1919, however, he had his own lithography press and stones in Santa Fe and did much of his own printing. See Ina Sizer Cassidy, "Prints," *New Mexico Magazine* 24 (January 1945): 24.

11. Pearson obituary, *New York Times*, 1 May 1958.

12. No checklist of this exhibition survives in the archives of the Museum of Fine Arts (hereafter, MFA). A brief account with mention of some titles is found in "Exhibit by a Master," *El Palacio* 5, no. 22 (28 December 1918): 366–67.

13. The Museum of Fine Arts is a division of the Museum of New Mexico, a state institution. When opened in 1917, it was first called the Fine Arts Gallery; subsequently, even in museum publications, the names Fine Arts Museum and Museum of Fine Arts were used interchangeably. Regardless of date, I will hereafter refer to the museum as the *Museum of Fine Arts*.

14. Fifty-nine of Sandzen's lithographs and woodcuts were included in an exhibition at the MFA in January 1919.

15. For Sandzen's work as an artist-lithographer, see Greenough, *Graphic Work of Birger Sandzen*; and O'Neill and Foreman, *Prairie Print Makers*.

16. Walt Kuhn to Walter Pach, 12 December 1912, reprinted in *1913 Armory Show, 50th Anniversary Exhibition*, 159.

17. The artists of The Eight were Arthur B. Davies, William J. Glackens, Robert Henri, Ernest Lawson, George B. Luks, Maurice B. Prendergast, Everett Shinn, and John Sloan. All but Shinn were later members of the Association of American Painters and Sculptors; Davies was president.

18. Coke, *Taos and Santa Fe*, 39.

19. Sloan, Davey, and B. J. O. Nordfeldt were elected associate members of the Taos Society of Artists in 1921; Sandzen and Gustave Baumann were elected associate members in 1922. In his report as secretary (1920–1921), Walter Ufer urged a broadening of the TSA's membership: "It was very difficult to get our exhibition into New York and Chicago among the dealers because our past exhibitions were not of high enough standard" (White, *Taos Society*, 72).

20. Bellows did not enter this lithograph in his record books and only two impressions are known. Lauris Mason, in her catalogue of Bellows's lithographs, suggests that it was done circa 1919 [Mason 70], but an earlier date is more likely. It does not appear to have been printed by Bolton Brown, who first printed for Bellows in December 1918 or early in 1919.

21. Coke, *Nordfeldt The Painter*, 32–33.

22. Ibid., 51.

23. Jonson, quoted by Coke, ibid., 65.

24. See Seward, *Metalplate Lithography for Artists and Draftsmen*.

25. J. B. Jackson, in *Gustave Baumann Centennial*, n.p.

26. Garoffolo, "Gustave Baumann," 37.

27. Ibid., 40.

28. Biographical data sheet in clipping files, MFA.

29. Truettner, "Science and Sentiment," in Eldredge, Schimmel, and Truetter, *Art in New Mexico*, 28.

30. The plates for *Stringing the Bow* and three other etchings, drawn by Hennings in the early 1920s, were found in 1976 among the personal effects of the artist. Hennings also made eight lithographs in 1924 and 1925, all of which were printed by the Jahn and Ollier Lithographic Company in Chicago, where Hennings's brother-in-law, Joseph E. Yell, served as art director. For further information about Hennings's prints, see White, *E. Martin Hennings*.

31. Sloan, quoted in Morse, *John Sloan's Prints*, 255.

32. The five were Josef Bakos, Fremont Ellis, Wladyslaw Mruk, Williard Nash, and Will Shuster.

33. See Coke, "A Contrast of Styles."

CHAPTER 2

1. Coke, *Andrew Dasburg*, 25.

2. After publication in the magazine in 1925, the two woodblocks, *Taos Pueblo I*, and *Taos Pueblo II*, were put aside. In 1978 John Sommers handprinted limited editions from the unaltered blocks. See Adams, "Prints of Andrew Dasburg," 22–23.

3. Coke, in *Kenneth M. Adams*, 12, writes "that in every instance where an Adams lithograph and painting incorporate the same motif, the lithograph preceded the painting." Goff, in "Kenneth M. Adams," 52, is more accurate: "Adams frequently uses and re-uses the same subject, exploring its possibilities in lithography, oil, and watercolor over a period of years." As example, the painting *Benerisa Tafoya* dates from 1932, the lithograph *Benerisa* from 1960.

4. Adams's first lithographs were printed at the Western Lithographic Company in Wichita. His lithographs made during the 1930s were printed by George C. Miller in New York. In the 1950s his stones were printed by Elmer Schooley in Las Vegas, New Mexico.

5. In *Ward Lockwood* (1967), Loren Mozley states that Lockwood's painting *Taos Plaza* was painted in 1934 (p. 8) but does not provide the source of this information (the painting itself is undated). Mozley describes it as one of a "series of pictures in oil . . . [which were] usually painted during the winter. Times were hard. These were the years of the Depression and the long slow recovery from it. Spirits were remarkably high among the painters, and, forced to stay at home, they produced a lot of work" (p. 10). To accept the dates ascribed to the lithograph and the painting is to accept an interval of about five years between them.

6. Duffy, *Howard Cook*, 17.

7. Cook, in "Autobiographical Notes" (unpublished), Roswell Museum and Art Center; quoted by Janet A. Flint, ibid., 35.

8. Ibid., 18.

9. Zigrosser, *World of Art and Museums*, 94.

10. Zigrosser, *Artist in America*, 193.

11. See Duffy, *Howard Cook;* and Adams, "Howard Norton Cook."

12. Taylor, in Farmer, *Image of Urban Optimism*.

13. Lockwood, quoted in *Taos News*, 24 May 1962, 13.

14. See Gibson, *Santa Fe and Taos Colonies*, 66–67.

15. Spurlock, "Federal Support," 9–11. Spurlock quotes a number of Baumann's candid appraisals of individual artists.

16. Ibid., 10.

17. Ibid., 44. Baumann's comment refers to Kloss's work for the PWAP. Spurlock identifies ten New Mexico artists who made prints on the WPA/FAP: Kloss, Charles Barrows, Manville Chapman, Millard Everingham, Russell Vernon Hunter (who was the project's New Mexico director), Josef Imhof, Zena Kavin, Juanita Lantz, Lloyd Moylan, and Harold W. West.

18. Kloss to Adams, 9 June 1990.

19. Ibid.

20. See Watrous, *Century of American Printmaking*, 103–7.

21. Duffy, *Howard Cook*, 23.

22. Rönnebeck, a German-born artist, had studied sculpture in Munich and in Paris with Maillol and Bourdelle. He came to the United States in 1923 where his lithographs of New York subjects were printed by George C. Miller. According to Udall, *Modernist Painting*, 105, Rönnebeck visited Mabel Dodge Luhan in Taos in 1924 and 1925 at the urging of his friend Marsden Hartley. He later sent several lithographs to Zigrosser from Denver (15 December 1931): "They are of subjects 'round little old Santa Fé and, therefore, may not find much of an echo among N.Y. addicts. . . . I had to get something out of my system about these much loved regions" (Zigrosser papers, University of Pennsylvania). Rönnebeck was director of the Denver Art Museum, 1926–31.

23. Imhof, quoted by David Farmer in Farmer to Adams, 22 August 1988.

CHAPTER 3

1. Baro, *30 Years of American Printmaking*, 9.

2. Boll, Walch, and Wilson, *Albuquerque '50s*, 6.

3. For Yunkers's early years, see Johnson, *Adja Yunkers: Prints;* and Adams, *Adja Yunkers Woodcuts*.

4. Yunkers, quoted by Johnson, *Adja Yunkers*, n.p.

5. Werner Drewes and Louis Schanker, who had been making rich and complex color woodcuts in New York since the 1930s, were later joined by such artists as Will Barnet, Antonio Frasconi, Seong Moy, and Carol Summers. Gene Baro wryly observes that in the 1940s, "Renaissance was the customary, if excessive, word used to describe what was a moderate increase in printmaking activity among American artists" (Baro, *30 Years*, 8).

6. Yunkers to Jonson, 14 December 1948. This and all subsequent references to the Yunkers-Jonson correspondence are to letters in the Jonson archives, UNM Art Museum.

7. Yunkers wrote Jonson, 5 February 1948: "I wish to thank you for your interest and kindness in helping me get that job at the U of NM . . . [it means] so much to me and my wife—who by the way is going to have her baby in June in Albuquerque."

8. Yunkers to Lez Haas, then chairman of the UNM Art Department, 21 July 1948 (Jonson archives).

9. Johnson, *American Prints and Printmakers*, 91.

10. Yunkers, *Prints in the Desert*.

11. Jonson wrote Yunkers (27 November 1948) that he had brought up the matter of his appointment to the faculty several times "with no success." The faculty consensus, he reported, "is that we do not need and are in no position to add any further work in graphics . . . [and that] when and if an addition is made to the staff it will be a painter." In Yunkers's second summer at the university, he taught life drawing, not printmaking.

12. Yunkers to Jonson, 22 November 1950.

13. Other participants were Vincent Garoffolo, Herb Goldman, Elmer Gorman, Edwin Honig, and A. Jarrett. Each folio included a painting by a child, photographs by Jarrett and Goldman, and original prints by Garver, O'Hara, Walters, and Yunkers. It was, overall, a curiously uneven publication, housed in a handsome folio designed and printed by Yunkers, but with the essays and poetry printed by multilith on cheap paper, evidence of precarious financing.

14. For technical information on O'Hara's method, see Antreasian and Adams, *Tamarind Book of Lithography*, sect. 15.22, 406.

15. Black to Adams, 28 March 1990.

16. See Boll, Walch, and Wilson, *Albuquerque '50s*.

17. Schooley to Adams, 22 March 1990.

18. Schooley printed for Kenneth Adams, Agnes Tait, Chuzo Tamotzu, Ila McAfee, and Theodore van Soelen, among others.

19. *Albuquerque Journal*, 12 October 1986.

20. Schooley, in the checklist of an exhibition at the Governor's Gallery, Santa Fe, 1981.

21. See Castleman, *American Impressions*, 56–57.

22. This statement in the flier "Transcendental Painting Group" is signed by the group's nine founding members: Jonson, Lumpkins, Bisttram, Robert Gribbroek, Lawren Harris, Florence Miller, Agnes Pelton, H. Towner Pierce, and Stuart Walker.

23. Lumpkins, in an exhibition announcement, Barn Gallery, Santa Fe, June 1961 (MFA clipping files).

24. Lumpkins, quoted by Wilson in Boll, Walch, and Wilson, *Albuquerque '50s*, 15.

25. A thirteenth exhibition was held at the State Fair art gallery in Albuquerque in 1960, but apparently was not shown at the Fine Arts Museum in Santa Fe. See Ina Sizer Cassidy, "Annual Exhibition of Prints," *New Mexico Magazine* (March 1960): 12.

26. Photographs were also included in a number of the exhibitions, and watercolors were included in the twelfth exhibition in 1959.

27. Printmaking in Colorado Springs had long been linked to Santa Fe and Taos. Ward Lockwood was the first to offer courses in lithography at the Broadmoor Art Academy in 1932. Beginning in 1936, Lawrence Barrett collaborated with visiting artists, among them Davey and Cook. See Adams, *American Lithographers*, 111–15, 167–70; Adams, "Lawrence Barrett"; and *Pikes Peak Vision*, 56, 71–77.

28. In the first annual exhibition (February 1947), 40 of the 47 artists worked either in Santa Fe or Taos; in the second (November-December 1947), 27 of 35; and in the third (December 1949), 28 of 38.

29. Moskowitz's lithographs were published as illustrations in John Collier, *Patterns and Ceremonials*.

30. Other Santa Fe artists who exhibited prints at the MFA between 1947 and 1959: Charles Barrows, Elizabeth D. Breneiser, John A. Breneiser, Stanley G. Breneiser, Louie Ewing, Dorothy S. King, Karl Larsson, Bernique Longley, William Longley, Lon Megargee, Alfred Morang, Lloyd Moylan, Katharine Schlater, Eva Springer, Dorothy N. Stewart, Theodore Van Soelen, Norma Van Sweringen, and Harold W. West.

31. McAfee to Adams, 7 June 1990. Of her lithograph, *A Small Ranch*, McAfee writes: "A native woman looked at it once and said, 'Too small to make a living *off* of.' I intended to make a rich composition but felt it turned out too black—after I saw the print—no chance to make any corrections." The impression in the collection of Mr. and Mrs. Van Deren Coke is titled in pencil, "At Evening Time," possibly by a hand other than the artist's.

32. Cassidy, "Carlsbad Artist," *New Mexico Magazine* 27 (January 1949): 22.

33. Reed, in the preface of *Doel Reed Makes an Aquatint*.

34. James T. Forrest, quoted in Laine, "Doel Reed," 11.

35. Brooks, *John Sloan*, 219.

36. See Udall, *Modernist Painting in New Mexico*, 173–76.

146

37. Mitchell Wilder, quoted in Boll, Walch, and Wilson, *Albuquerque '50s*, 18.

38. Black, "Criticism of Fiesta Show," 6–7.

39. Ibid.

40. Beulah Johnson and Thomas Wilson.

41. Ashton, quoted in Boll, Walch, and Wilson, *Albuquerque '50s*, 43.

42. *Santa Fe New Mexican*, 29 May 1960. Beginning in mid-May, letters and news reports about Black's dismissal and its aftermath appeared almost daily in the *New Mexican* (and frequently in the *Albuquerque Journal*). See clipping files, MFA.

CHAPTER 4

1. Adams, *American Lithographers*, 160.

2. Kline, quoted in Hess, "History, Style and Money," 29.

3. Intaglio printmaking is a generic term for processes that include etching, drypoint, aquatint, engraving, soft-ground, etc. It came into use in the 1940s and 1950s to describe prints in which these processes were combined.

4. New Mexico's universities did not participate in the intaglio printmaking movement of the late 1940s and 1950s. Intaglio workshops were belatedly established at UNM in 1971 and at NMSU in 1978; see chapter 5.

5. See Adams, *American Lithographers*, 178.

6. Ibid., 160.

7. For Lowengrund and Grosman, see ibid., 182–92.

8. Wayne, "To Restore the Art."

9. For the genesis and early history of TLW, see Adams, *American Lithographers*, 181–82, 193–203.

10. I met June Wayne at Lynton Kistler's Los Angeles lithography workshop in 1948. In 1954, I left my teaching position at UCLA to accept an appointment at the University of Kentucky; in 1958–59, when Wayne and I first discussed the possibility of a new workshop in Los Angeles, I was head of the art department at the University of Florida. For my work in lithography, see Van Deren Coke, *Clinton Adams*.

11. See Lewis, *Garo Antreasian*.

12. O'Hara and I met for the first time at Tamarind. He later suggested my appointment as dean at UNM, where I was able to assist the development of lithography in New Mexico.

13. Antreasian and I also continued to supervise Tamarind's advanced printer-training program in Los Angeles throughout the 1960s.

14. Printer fellows who complete Tamarind's demanding program of professional training receive certification as "Tamarind Master Printer" (TMP). Characteristically, they then accept positions in existing workshops or establish workshops of their own. For Tamarind after 1960, see Gedeon, "Tamarind: Los Angeles to Albuquerque"; for a list of workshops, see Schnelker, "American Print Workshops."

15. The substantial grant from the Ford Foundation (which came to UNM via TLW), provided funds to move the workshop from Los Angeles to Albuquerque, acquire a building, hire a staff, and support a transitional program of artist residencies.

16. The three who came from Los Angeles were John Sommers (studio manager), Harry Westlund, and Tracy S. White; joining the program in Albuquerque were John Butke (a former printer fellow in Los Angeles), W. Wayne Kimball, Jr., and Wayne H. Simpkins.

17. *Contract printing* (sometimes called custom printing) is work done for payment; the artist is quoted a price based upon the complexity and amount of work to be done, and the edition is delivered upon completion. *Publishing* involves financial participation in a project by the printmaking workshop and/or the artist's agent or gallery; the artist does not pay for the workshop's services, but assigns a percentage of income from sales to the publisher. Publishing arrangements are highly variable.

18. This and two following paragraphs are restated from Adams, *Fritz Scholder Lithographs.*

19. O'Keeffe, in conversation with the author, Abiquiu, New Mexico, 29 September 1978.

20. For Dasburg's working methods, see Adams, "Andrew Dasburg," 20–21.

21. Sommers, quoting Dasburg, ibid., 21.

22. Traugott, "John Sommers," 7.

23. Ackerman, "Earl Stroh," 10.

24. Nadler to Adams, 29 March 1990.

CHAPTER 5

1. Moore, in *Garo Z. Antreasian: A Retrospective,* 8.

2. This process, sometimes called the "rainbow roll," makes use of two or more inks carried simultaneously on the printer's roller; these inks blend together to produce a gradation of tones or colors. Although developed in the nineteenth century, blended inking had seldom been used in contemporary lithography before it was employed as the thematic text of Antreasian's *Quantum* suite (1966) and, with powerful effect, in Jasper Johns's *Color Numeral Series* (1968–69).

3. Fidler to Adams, 20 December 1989.

4. Tubis to Adams, 4 April 1990.

5. Tubis to Adams, 19 March 1990.

6. Sewards to Adams, 10 April 1990.

7. Wayne Enstice and Emile Webrile in *A Gift of Time,* n.p.

8. To offer high school courses in etching and lithography, as McCulloch did, is unusual in the United States; to my knowledge, it was then unique in New Mexico.

9. I had taught a similar course at UCLA in the early 1950s in association with Lynton Kistler, who printed the students' editions.

10. See Jones, "American Lithography and Tamarind," 248–49; and Fine, *Gemini G.E.L.*

11. Ron Adams, quoted in *Santa Fe New Mexican*, 30 March 1984.

12. Arber's first project was the "Goatshed Editions," commissioned by the Bob Tomlinson Gallery in Albuquerque, and named for the goat shed in which Arber then housed his old Fuchs & Lang press. The nine artists were John Connell, Rebecca Davis, Frank Ettenberg, deWayne Harrison, Reg Loving, Eugene Newman, Sam Scott, Beth Ames Swartz, and Richard Thompson.

13. Stevens, in *Woody Gwyn* (1988).

14. Stevens quotes Rainer Maria Rilke, ibid.

15. Hamilton, who completed certification as a Tamarind Master Printer in 1978, founded Cuervo Creative Papers in 1982 and continued its operation for four years thereafter, during which time he supplied handmade paper for projects in several printmaking workshops, but more frequently collaborated directly with artists in the making of unique or multiple cast-paper pieces, including a series of large pieces cast for Judy Chicago, later painted by the artist. Hamilton remains active as a painter and printmaker.

16. Peterson, in *Waldrum: The Etchings*, n.p.

17. Ibid.

18. See Peterson, "Harold Joe Waldrum Makes a Linocut," 52.

19. Booth, in conversation, 19 January 1990.

20. Westlund continued operation of Serigraphics until 1984, collaborating with Nick Abdalla, Earl Biss, R. C. Gorman, Jerry Ingram, Susan Linnell, John Nieto, and Arthur Sussman, among others. After a five-year interval, Westlund established a new workshop, Centipede Custom Serigraph, in 1989.

21. The phrase is James McNeill Whistler's (*The Gentle Art of Making Enemies*, 1890).

22. Antreasian, in conversation, 15 January 1989.

23. Phillips obituary, *Tamarind Papers* 10 (1987), 43.

24. Brown, *Lithography*, 7.

25. See Ruth E. Fine, "Bigger, Brighter, Bolder: American Lithography since the Second World War," in Gilmour, *Lasting Impressions*, 257–82.

26. The other artists included in *Seis Santeros* are Charles Carrillo, Ramón López, Eluid Martínez, and Anita Romero Jones. The tin work that decorates the cover of the portfolio is by Bonafacio Sandoval.

27. The prints included in *Artists' Impressions* are printed in a single press run (most in black ink) on a sheet 305 x 305 mm (12 x 12 in); among the artists are

Clinton Adams, Garo Antreasian, Walter Askin, William Brice, Larry Brown, Robert Colescott, James Davis, James Drake, Gendron Jensen, Roberto Juárez, George McNeil, Italo Scanga, and Jaune Quick-to-See Smith.

28. McCulloch, in conversation, 5 April 1990.
29. Britko, in conversation, 2 March 1990.
30. Pound, in *The Spirit of Romance* (1910).

150

BIBLIOGRAPHY

This effort to piece together a cohesive history of printmaking in New Mexico is admittedly incomplete. It is my hope that the imbalances in what I have written may lead other writers to fill in many spaces that are now blank. Most needed are studies of individual artists. Thus far, few have been subjects of satisfactory catalogues raisonnés; the exhibition catalogues and checklists that have been preserved frequently omit essential data. Although the record improves after 1970, it is still in many ways lacking.

The historic hostility of the state's major newspapers—in particular the *Albuquerque Journal* and the *Santa Fe New Mexican*—toward progressive currents in art and their failure to publish serious critical reviews of exhibitions has deprived (and often continues to deprive) artists and historians of an essential chronicle. For knowledge of past events we depend heavily upon the brief reports published in *El Palacio*, a journal published by the Museum of New Mexico, and upon the columns, "Art and Artists of New Mexico," written by Ina Sizer Cassidy for the *New Mexico Magazine* over a period of thirty-one years. George Fitzpatrick, Cassidy's colleague at the magazine, correctly described her as "not so much an art critic as an encourager of art." While her chatty style can frustrate the researcher who seeks factual information, her writings nonetheless provide a sympathetic record of much that might otherwise have been lost.

Fortunately, a substantial number of primary sources are at hand: in Santa Fe, the archives of the Museum of New Mexico and the clipping files of the Museum of Fine Arts; in Taos, the archives of the Harwood Foundation; and in Albuquerque, the Jonson archives of the University Art Museum and the Tamarind archives (housed in the UNM Fine Arts Library). The papers of a number of New Mexican artists have been donated to the Archives of American Art, Smithsonian Institution (among them, the papers of Tamotzu Chuzo, Howard Cook, Andrew Dasburg, Herbert [Buck] Dunton, Russell Vernon Hunter, Raymond Jonson, Barbara Latham, Ward Lockwood, B. J. O. Nordfeldt, Will Shuster, and Walter Ufer). Such materials are an invitation to scholars. The master's theses written by Kate M. Duncan (on Cady Wells) and William H. Spurlock, II (on federal support for the visual arts in New Mexico) suggest what is possible when that invitation is accepted within our universities. Elizabeth Jones-Popescu's Ph.D. dissertation will remain important as a study of Tamarind.

With two exceptions (reports published in newspapers and Cassidy's columns in *New Mexico Magazine*) the list below includes all books and articles cited in the notes.

Ackerman, Esther. "Earl Stroh: Tough Views on Art," *Artlines* (October 1981), 9–10.

Adams, Clinton. *American Lithographers, 1900–1960: The Artists and Their Printers*. Albuquerque: University of New Mexico Press, 1983.

———. "Lawrence Barrett: Colorado's Prophet of Stone," *Artspace* (Fall 1978): 38–43.

———. "Howard Norton Cook: The Graphic Work," *New Mexico Studies in the Fine Arts* 4 (1979): 11–15.

———. "The Prints of Andrew Dasburg: A Complete Catalogue," *Tamarind Papers* 4 (Winter 1980–81): 18–25.

———. *Fritz Scholder Lithographs*. Boston: New York Graphic Society, 1975.

———. "Introduction," *Adja Yunkers Woodcuts, 1927–1966* [exhibition catalogue]. New York: Associated American Artists, 1988.

Adja Yunkers Prints: 1942–1982 [exhibition catalogue]. Albion, Mich.: Albion College, 1982.

Alexander Masley Abstractions [exhibition catalogue]. Albuquerque: Jonson Gallery, 1989.

Antreasian, Garo, with Clinton Adams. *The Tamarind Book of Lithography: Art & Techniques*. New York: Abrams, 1971.

Ashton, Dore. "Adja Yunkers: His Prints," *Bulletin of Pasadena Art Institute* 2 (October 1951): 11–15.

Baro, Gene. *30 Years of American Printmaking*. Brooklyn: Brooklyn Museum, 1976.

Beall, Karen F., et al. *American Prints in the Library of Congress: A Catalogue of the Collection*. Baltimore: Johns Hopkins Press, 1970.

Black, Frederick. "A Criticism of the 1957 Fiesta Show at the Museum of New Mexico and Suggestions on Museum Policy" [unpublished report to Wayne L. Mauzy], 1957.

Boll, Deborah, Peter Walch, and MaLin Wilson. *Albuquerque '50s* [exhibition catalogue]. Albuquerque: University of New Mexico Art Museum, 1989.

Brooks, Van Wyck. *John Sloan: A Painter's Life*. New York: Dutton, 1955.

Brown, Bolton. *Lithography*. New York: FitzRoy Carrington, 1923.

Cady Wells, 1904–1954 [exhibition catalogue]. San Francisco: California Palace of the Legion of Honor, 1956.

Catalogue of the Etched Work of Peter Moran. New York: Frederick Keppel & Co., 1888.

Coke, Van Deren. *Clinton Adams: A Retrospective Exhibition of Lithographs* [exhibition catalogue]. Albuquerque: University of New Mexico Art Museum, 1973.

————. *Kenneth M. Adams: A Retrospective Exhibition* [exhibition catalogue]. Albuquerque: University of New Mexico Press, 1964.

————. *Andrew Dasburg*. Albuquerque: University of New Mexico Press, 1979.

————. "A Contrast of Styles: Two Lithographs by Willard Nash," *Tamarind Papers* 13 (1990): 82–84.

————. *The Drawings of Andrew Dasburg* [exhibition catalogue]. Albuquerque: University of New Mexico Art Museum, 1966.

————. *Nordfeldt the Painter*. Albuquerque: University of New Mexico Press, 1972.

————. *Taos and Santa Fe: The Artist's Environment, 1882–1942*. Albuquerque: University of New Mexico Press, for Amon Carter Museum of Western Art and Art Gallery, University of New Mexico, 1963.

Collier, John. *Patterns and Ceremonials of the Indians of the Southwest*. New York: Dutton, 1949.

D'Emilio, Sandra. *The Alcove Show: Gustave Baumann, Ernest L. Blumenschein, William Penhallow Henderson, Gene Kloss, Ernest Knee, and John Sloan* [exhibition catalogue]. Santa Fe: Museum of New Mexico, 1988.

De Kooning, Elaine. "New Mexico," *Art in America* 49 (1961): 56–59.

DeLong, Lea R. *Nature's Forms/Nature's Forces: The Art of Alexandre Hogue*. Tulsa: Philbrook Art Center and the University of Oklahoma Press, ca. 1984.

Dispenza, Joseph, and Louise Turner. *Will Shuster: A Santa Fe Legend*. Santa Fe: Museum of New Mexico Press, 1989.

Doel Reed Makes an Aquatint. Santa Fe: Museum of New Mexico Press, 1965.

Duffy, Betty and Douglas. *The Graphic Work of Howard Cook: A Catalogue Raisonné*. Bethesda, Maryland: Bethesda Art Gallery, 1984.

Duncan, Kate M. "Cady Wells: The Personal Vision." Master's thesis, University of New Mexico, 1967.

Eldredge, Charles C. *Ward Lockwood, 1894–1963*. Lawrence: University of Kansas Museum of Art, 1974

Eldredge, Charles C., Julie Schimmel, and William H. Truettner. *Art in New Mexico, 1900–1945: Paths to Taos and Santa Fe*. Washington: National Musuem of American Art, 1986.

Farmer, Jane M. *The Image of Urban Optimism* [exhibition catalogue]. Introduction by Joshua C. Taylor. Washington: Smithsonian Institution, 1977.

Field, Richard S., et al. *American Prints 1900–1950*. New Haven: Yale University Art Gallery, 1983.

Fine, Ruth E. *Gemini G.E.L.: Art and Collaboration*. Washington and New York: National Gallery of Art and Abbeville Press, 1984.

Frederick O'Hara: A Retrospective Exhibition [exhibition checklist]. Roswell Museum and Art Center, 1979.

Freundlich, August L. *Federico Castellón, His Graphic Works, 1936–1971*. Syracuse: College of Visual and Performing Arts, Syracuse University, 1978.

Garoffolo, Vincent. "Gustave Baumann," in *New Mexico Artists*, 33–48. Albuquerque: University of New Mexico Press, 1958.

Garo Z. Antreasian: A Retrospective 1942–1987. Essay by James Moore. Albuquerque: Albuquerque Museum, 1988.

Gedeon, Lucinda H. "Tamarind: From Los Angeles to Albuquerque," *Grunwald Center Studies V* (1984). Los Angeles: Grunwald Center for the Graphic Arts, UCLA, 1984.

Gene Kloss Etchings. Explanatory text by Phillips Kloss. Santa Fe: Sunstone Press, 1981.

Gibson, Arrell Morgan. *The Santa Fe and Taos Colonies: Age of the Muses, 1900–1942*. Norman: University of Oklahoma Press, 1983.

A Gift of Time: 20th Anniversary, The Artist-in-Residence Program [exhibition catalogue]. Roswell Museum and Art Center, 1987.

Gilmour, Pat, ed. *Lasting Impressions: Lithography as Art*. Canberra: Australian National Gallery, 1988.

Goff, Lloyd Lózes. "Kenneth M. Adams," in *New Mexico Artists*, 49–64. Albuquerque: University of New Mexico Press, 1958.

Goldman, Judith. *American Prints: Process & Proofs* [exhibition catalogue]. New York: Harper & Row for the Whitney Museum of American Art, 1981.

Greenough, Charles Pelham, III. *The Graphic Work of Birger Sandzen*. Lindborg, Kansas: Bethany College, 1952.

Gustave Baumann Centennial: A Retrospective Exhibition [exhibition catalogue]. Santa Fe: Museum of New Mexico, 1981.

Haas, Lez. "Frederick O'Hara," *New Mexico Quarterly* 21 (Autumn 1951): 294–99.

Handbook of the Collections, 1917–1974. Santa Fe: Museum of Fine Arts, Museum of New Mexico, 1974.

Here and Now: 35 Artists in New Mexico [exhibition catalogue]. Albuquerque: Albuquerque Museum, 1980.

Hess, Thomas B. "Prints: Where History, Style and Money Meet," *Art News* (January 1972): 29.

Horgan, Paul. *Peter Hurd: A Portrait Sketch from Life*. Austin: University of Texas Press for the Amon Carter Museum of Western Art, [1965].

Hurst, Tricia. "Influenced by The Masters," *Southwest Art* (March 1975): 44–49.

Johnson, Una E. *American Prints and Printmakers*. Garden City, N.Y.: Doubleday & Co., 1980.

Johnson, Una E., and Jo Miller. *Adja Yunkers: Prints 1927–1967*. Brooklyn: Brooklyn Museum, 1969.

Jones-Popescu, Elizabeth. "American Lithography and Tamarind Lithography Workshop/Tamarind Institute, 1900–1980." Ph.D. dissertation, University of New Mexico, 1980.

Laine, Don. "Doel Reed, An Artist for All Time," *High Country Profile* 10 (March 1985): 11.

Leeper, John Palmer. "Adja Yunkers," in *New Mexico Artists*, 65–81. Albuquerque: University of New Mexico Press, 1952.

Lewis, Louise M. *Garo Antreasian* [exhibition catalogue]. Albuquerque: University of New Mexico, 1973.

Light and Color, Images from New Mexico: Masterpieces from the Collection of the Museum of Fine Arts, Museum of New Mexico [exhibition catalogue]. Introduction by Norman R. Geske. Kansas City, Mo.: Mid-America Arts Alliance, 1981.

Luis Jimenez: Sculpture, Drawings and Prints [exhibition catalogue]. Las Cruces: University Art Gallery, New Mexico State University, 1977.

Made in California: An Exhibition of Five Workshops [exhibition catalogue]. Los Angeles: Grunwald Graphic Arts Foundation, UCLA, 1971.

Made in New Mexico [exhibition brochure]. Essay by Rosalind Constable. Santa Fe: Museum of Fine Arts, 1976.

Mason, Lauris, with Joan Ludman. *The Lithographs of George Bellows: A Catalogue Raisonné*. Millwood, N.Y.: KTO Press, 1977.

Meigs, John, ed. *Peter Hurd: The Lithographs*. Lubbock, Tex.: Baker Gallery Press, 1968.

Monthan, Doris. *R. C. Gorman: The Lithographs*. Flagstaff, Ariz.: Northland Press, 1978.

Morse, Peter. *John Sloan's Prints: A Catalogue Raisonné of the Etchings, Lithographs and Posters*. New Haven: Yale University Press, 1969.

Myers, Jane, and Linda Ayres. *George Bellows: The Artist and His Lithographs, 1916–1924*. Fort Worth: Amon Carter Museum, 1988.

The New Deal in the Southwest: Arizona and New Mexico [exhibition catalogue]. Essay by Peter Bermingham. Tucson: University of Arizona Museum of Art, 1980.

1913 Armory Show, 50th Anniversary Exhibition, 1963 [exhibition catalogue]. New York and Utica: Henry Street Settlement and Munson-Williams-Proctor Institute, 1963.

O'Neill, Barbara Thompson, and George C. Foreman, with Howard W. Ellington. *The Prairie Print Makers*. Topeka: Kansas Arts Commission, 1981.

Paintings by Barbara Latham [exhibition catalogue]. Roswell: Roswell Museum and Art Center, 196–.

Peet, Phyllis. *American Women of the Etching Revival* [exhibition catalogue]. Atlanta: High Museum of Art, 1988.

Peña, Lydia M. *The Life and Times of Agnes Tait, 1894–1981*. Arvada, Colo., and Roswell, N.M.: Arvada Center for Arts and Humanities and Roswell Museum and Art Center, 1984.

Pennell, Joseph, and E. R. Pennell. *Lithography and Lithographers, Some Chapters in the History of the Art*. London: T. Fisher Unwin, 1898. Rewritten, with the order of the author's names inverted on the title page, New York: Macmillan, 1915.

Peterson, William. "Harold Joe Waldrum Makes a Linocut," *Artspace* 13 (Winter 1988–89): 52–55.

Pikes Peak Vision: The Broadmoor Art Academy, 1919–1945 [exhibition catalogue]. Essay by Stanley L. Cuba with Elizabeth Cunningham. Colorado Springs: Colorado Springs Fine Arts Center, 1989.

A Policy Statement: The Fine Arts Museum of New Mexico (Bulletin No. 1). Santa Fe: Museum of New Mexico, 1962.

Randall Davey [exhibition catalogue]. Santa Fe: Museum of New Mexico, 1957.

Randall Davey [exhibition catalogue]. Roswell: Roswell Museum and Art Center, 1963.

Robertson, Edna. *Gerald Cassidy, 1869–1934* [exhibition catalogue]. Santa Fe: Museum of New Mexico, 1977.

Robertson, Edna, and Sarah Nestor. *Artists of the Canyons and Caminos: Santa Fe, The Early Years*. Peregrine Smith, 1976.

Roderick Mead, 1900–1972 [*sic*]: *A Retrospective Exhibition* [exhibition catalogue]. Midland, Tex.: Museum of the Southwest, 1972.

Schimmel, Julie. *The Art and Life of W. Herbert Dunton, 1878–1936*. Austin: University of Texas Press for Stark Museum of Art, 1984.

Schnelker, Rebecca, comp. "American Print Workshops: A Survey," *Tamarind Papers* 12 (1989): 86–94.

Schnelker, Rebecca, ed. *Tamarind Lithographs: A Complete Catalogue of Lithographs*

Printed at Tamarind Institute, 1970–1979. Albuquerque: Tamarind Institute, 1980.

Seward, C. A. *Metalplate Lithography for Artists and Draftsmen.* New York: Pencil Points Press, 1931.

Spurlock, William H., II. "Federal Support for the Visual Arts in the State of New Mexico, 1933–1943." Master's thesis, University of New Mexico, 1974.

Stewart, Janet. "Depression Art of Arizona and New Mexico," *Southwest Art* (September 1981): 109–15.

Tamarind Suite Fifteen [exhibition catalogue]. Essay by Gustave von Groschwitz. Albuquerque: Tamarind Institute, in association with the University of New Mexico Art Museum, 1977.

Tamarind: 25 Years [exhibition catalogue]. Essay by Carter Ratcliff. Albuquerque: Tamarind Institute, 1985.

"Transcendental Painting Group" [flier]. Santa Fe: Transcendental Painting Group, n.d. [1938].

Traugott, Joseph, "John Sommers," *Tamarind Papers* 11 (1988): 6–9.

Udall, Sharyn R. *Modernist Painting in New Mexico, 1913–1936.* Albuquerque: University of New Mexico Press, 1984.

Waldrum: The Etchings [exhibition catalogue]. Introduction by William Peterson. Santa Fe: Gerald Peters Gallery, 1985.

Ward Lockwood: A Retrospective Exhibition of Paintings, Prints and Drawings [exhibition catalogue]. Austin: University Art Museum of the University of Texas, 1967.

Watrous, James. *A Century of American Printmaking, 1880–1980.* Madison: University of Wisconsin Press, 1984.

Wayne, June C. "To Restore the Art of the Lithograph in the United States." Proposal submitted to the Ford Foundation, 1958. Tamarind archives, University of New Mexico.

White, Robert R. *The Lithographs and Etchings of E. Martin Hennings.* Santa Fe: Museum of New Mexico Press, [1978].

White, Robert R., ed. *The Taos Society of Artists.* Albuquerque: University of New Mexico Press, 1983.

Will Shuster: A Santa Fe Legend [exhibition checklist]. Santa Fe: Museum of Fine Arts, 1989.

Witt, David. *The Taos Artists: A Historical Narrative and Biographical Dictionary.* Colorado Springs: Ewell Fine Arts, 1984.

Woody Gwyn [exhibition catalogue]. Essay by Mark Stevens. Santa Fe: Gerald Peters Gallery, 1988.

Yunkers, Adja, ed. *Prints in the Desert.* Alameda, N.M.: 1950.

Zigrosser, Carl. *The Artist in America: Contemporary Printmakers*. New York: Alfred A. Knopf, 1942. Reprinted, New York: Hacker Art Books, 1978.

———. "Howard Cook," in *New Mexico Artists*, 117–31. Albuquerque: University of New Mexico Press, 1958.

———. "Prints in the Southwest," *Southwest Review* 26 (Winter 1941): 188–202.

———. *A World of Art and Museums*. Philadelphia: Art Alliance Press, 1975.

INDEX

Except for the plates, which are on unnumbered pages, all references are to page numbers.

Abbey, Edward, 69
Abdalla, Nick, 91, 149; *Nude in Red Kimono, 95*
Abrams, Jane, 91, 104–6, 108, 111
   Fumbling at the Speed of Light, 106
Acoma Hawk V (Oliveira), 98, *99*
Acoma Mesa I (McNeil), 98, *100*
Adams, Ben Q., 80, 102, 123
Adams, Clinton, 72, 76, 80, 114, 130, 147, 150
   Strata, 76, 79
Adams, Kenneth M., 27, 38, 57, 66, 73, 143, 145
   Adobe Bricklayer, 30
   Harvest, 31
Adams, Ron, 115–18; *Profile in Blue, Plate XI, 118*
Adobe and Wild Plum (Reed), 66, *67*
Adobe Bricklayer (Kenneth M. Adams), *30*
Ahern, Mary, 111
Albers, Josef, 57
Aman-Jean, Edmond François, 4
Anderson, Donald B., 108
Antreasian, Garo, 72–73, 76, 84, 100–103, 106, 124–27, 148, 150
   Bebek II, Plate XIII, 127
   Plums, 103, 104

Untitled 72–121, 103, 105
App, Timothy, *Untitled,* 130, *135*
Arber and Son Editions, 115
Arber, Robert, 115
Armory Show, 3–4, 8, 10
Art Students League of New York, 114
Artist and Model (Johansen), 115, *117*
Artist's Equity, 68
Artists' Impressions (suite), 136
Artspace (magazine), 139
Ashton, Dore, 68–69
Askin, Walter, 150
Association of American Painters and Sculptors, 8
Atelier 17, 47–48, 71

B. Print (Jonson), 73, *76*
Baby Sitter, The (Snidow), *89*
Backstage (SFO) (Moyano), 118, *120*
Baker, Lynn, 87
Bakos, Josef, 18
Balink, Henry C., *Chief Paccaneh,* 18, *20*
Ballinger, Max, 53
Barnet, Will, 145
Baro, Gene, 47, 145
Barrett, Lawrence, 57, 63, 71, 146

Barrow, Thomas, 90; *Task Mask, Plate XV,* 130

Barrows, Charles, 144, 146

Baumann, Gustave, 16–18, 38, 57, 68, 73, 139, 142
Morning Sun, 17, *plate I*
San Geronimo—Taos, frontispiece, 16

Bebek II (Antreasian), *Plate XIII,* 127

Bellows, George, 10, 142
Well at Quevado (drawing), 10–12, *13*
Well at Quevado (lithograph), 10–12, *13*

Benrimo, Tom, 87

Berg, Tom, 130; *Dark Adirondack, 134*

Berninghaus, Oscar, 1; *Street Scene, Taos,* 4, *5*

Biss, Earl, 149

Bisttram, Emil, 27, 146; *Peace,* 27, *29*

Black, Frederick, 66–68; *Regatta: The Start, 68*

Blanchard, Robert, 123

Bleha, Bernard, 115

Block Print IV (Sihvonen), *60*

Blue Spirit (Hammond), *92*

Blumenschein, Ernest L., 1, 44

Blumenschein, Helen, 63–64;
Untitled (Ranchos de Taos), 65

Booth, Judy, 124

Botanical Layout: Peony (Hahn), *94*

Brach, Paul, *Sandia,* 98, *101*

Brady, Robert, 118

Breneiser, Elizabeth D., 146

Breneiser, John A., 146

Breneiser, Stanley G., 146

Brice, William, 150

Britko, Stephen, 118, 138

Broadmoor Art Academy, 146

Brown, Bolton, 10–11, 16, 130, 142

Brown, Larry, 150

Buffalo, Benjamin, 108

Burr, George Elbert, 40

Burro Train, New Mexico, A (Peter Moran), *2, 3*

Butke, John, 148

Bywaters, Jerry, 44

Campbell, Clayton, 90

Cannon, T. C., 80

Carlyle, Thomas, 139

Carrillo, Charles, 149

Cassidy, Gerald, 4, 16
Portrait of Mrs. M., 4, *6*
Sand Storm, 4, *7*

Cassidy, Ina Sizer, 64, 151

Castellón, Federico, *Taos Tryst,* 40, *41*

Cather, Willa, 32

Cemetery (Dwight), *36*

Centipede Custom Graphic, 149

Cézanne, Paul, 15, 27

Chapman, Manville, 144

Charlot, Jean, 40, 47

Chicago, Judy, 98, 149; *Creation, The, Plate XII,* 124

Chief Paccaneh (Balink), 18, *20*

chromolithography, 1–2

Church at Canyoncito, The (Dickerson), *17*

Church at Ranchos de Taos (Pearson), *8*

Cincinnati Art Museum, biennial exhibitions at, 72

Cinco Pintores, Los, 18–22

Clout (Hammersley), *Plate XVI,* 130

Cohoe, Grey, 108

Coke, Van Deren, 73

Colescott, Robert, 150

Colorado Springs Fine Arts Center, 114

Comanche Gap IV (O'Hara), *50, 51*

Connell, John, 149

Contemporaries Graphic Art Centre, 72

Cook, Howard, 32–33, 35–36, 40, 57, 73, 108, 139, 146
Lobo, The, 35
Morning Smokes, Taos Pueblo, 34

Cook, The (Van Soelen), *63*

Costello, Michael, 115–18

Couse, E. Irving, 1

Creation, The (Chicago), *plate XII*, 124

Crossbearer (Nash), 22, *23*

Crucifixion (Nordfeldt), *15*

Cuervo Creative Papers, 124

Cuno, Theodore, 60

Custom Etching Studio, 123–24

Dark Adirondack (Berg), *134*

Dasburg, Andrew, 25–27, 32–33, 40, 68, 83–86
  Ranchos Valley I, 84, *85*
  Taos Pueblo I, 25, *26*

Davey, Randall, 10, 57, 66, 68, 71, 142, 146
  Penitentes, 10, *12*
  Wet Day at the Track (Davey), 57, *58*

Davis, James, 150

Davis, Rebecca, 149

Dawn (Feinberg), *136*

de Kooning, Elaine, 52, 89

Descent of Discord (Phillips), *Plate XIV*, 127

Devon, Marjorie, 130

Dickerson, William, 16; *Church at Canyoncito, The*, *17*

Diebenkorn, Richard, 51–52, 72

Dodge, Mabel, 25, 32, 144

Douglass, Ralph, 60

Drake, James, 150

Drewes, Werner, 145

Dunton, Herbert (Buck), 1, 4

Duveneck, Frank, 3–4

Dwight, Mabel, *Cemetery*, *36*

Earth-World (Nauman), 115, *116*

Edge of Autumn (Scott), *91*

Eight, The, 10, 142

Ellis, Fremont, 143

Ellis, Robert M., 75, 91; *Rio Grande Gorge #16*, *96*

Envelope (Red Background) (Sarkisian), *Plate X*, 115

Ernst, Max, 18

Ettenberg, Frank, 149

Everingham, Millard, 144

Ewing, Louie H., 40, 146

Ewing, Robert A., 80

Farr, Helen, 59

Fechin, Nicolai, 25; *Mexican Girl*, 27, *28*

Federal Art Project, *See* Works Progress Administration (WPA)

Feinberg, Elen, 91; *Dawn*, *136*

Fidler, Spencer, 108; *Madness*, *109*

Fisher, Reginald, 66

Fitzpatrick, George, 151

Five Crosses (Hogue), 44, *45*

Fletcher, Frank Morley, 12

Forbis, Steve, 118–23; *Sharing Traditions*, *123*

Ford Foundation, 72, 76, 114, 148

Forum (magazine), 32

Francis, Sam, 55

Frasconi, Antonio, 145

Fumbling at the Speed of Light (Abrams), *106*

Garden of Folly, Series II (O'Hara), 51, *plate IV*

Garden Walk (Schooley), *54*, 55

Garfield, Duane R., 102

Garoffolo, Vincent, 145

Garver, Jack, 51, 68

Gash, Gail, *Shin Hanga III*, 127, *128*

Gateway (Lowney), *Plate IX*, 115

Gauguin, Paul, 48

Gemini, Ltd., 115

Geronimo of Taos (Imhof), 18, *21*

Glow Bugs (Schleeter), *61*

Goatshed Editions, 149

Goldman, Herbert, 145

Golem, The (Shapiro), 118, *121*

Gorman, Elmer, 145

Gorman, R. C., 80–83, 123, 149; *Taos Man*, *81*

Gran Quivira (Sandzen), 8, *9*

Grey Labyrinth (Nadler), 91, *97*

Gribbroek, Robert, 146

Grosman, Tatyana, 72

Grow, Ronald, 75

161

Guston, Philip, 53
Gwyn, Woody, *Interstate*, 118, *119*

Haas, Lez, 145
Haden, Seymour, 3
Hahn, Betty, 90; *Botanical Layout:
    Peony, 94*
Hall, Arthur W., 59
Hall, Norma Bassett, 59
Hambidge, Jay, 27
Hamilton, Russell, 118, 124, 149
Hammersley, Fred, 90; *Clout, Plate
    XVI, 130*
Hammond, Harmony, 90; *Blue Spirit,
    92*
Hand Graphics, Ltd., 115–18
Hanks, Steve, 118
Hare, David, 89
Harjo, Benjamin, Jr., 108
Harris, Lawren, 146
Harrison, deWayne, 149
Hartley, Marsden, 83, 144
Harvest (Kenneth M. Adams), *31*
Harvest at San Juan (Peter Moran), *3*
Harwood Foundation, 33
Hayter, Stanley William, 47, 53, 64,
    71
Hennings, E. Martin, 16, 143;
    Stringing the Bow, 18, *19*
Henri, Robert, 10
Higgins, Victor, 16
Highland High School, 114
Highlands University, 53–55
Hinds, Patrick Swazo, 80
Hoffman, Hans, 53
Hogue, Alexandre, *Five Crosses*, 44,
    45
Holden, Brenda, 108
Honig, Edwin, 145
Hoover, Ellison, *Untitled (Taos
    Pueblo), 40, 42*
Hopi Snake Dance, Walpi Mesa
    (Sloan), 10, *11*
Hunter, Russell Vernon, 40, 144
Hurd, Peter, 60–64, 68, 71; *Night
    Watchman, The, 60, 62*

Imhof, Josef A., 18, 44, 57, 73, 144
    Geronimo of Taos, 18, *21*
*Indian on Galloping Horse after
    Remington #2* (Scholder), *Plate VI*,
    80
Indians Forever (Scholder), 80
Ingram, Jerry, 149
Institute of American Indian Arts, 80,
    108
Interstate (Gwyn), 118, *119*

Jaramillo, Hazel, 115
Jarrett, Alfred, 145
Jeffers, Robinson, 25
Jensen, Gendron, 150
Jimenez, Luis, 118–23; *Snake and
    Eagle, 122, 123*
Johansen, Carl, *Artist and Model*,
    115, *117*
Johns, Jasper, 115, 148
Johnson, Beulah, 147
Johnson, Douglas, 90
Johnson, E. Dana, 66
Johnson, Gerald C., 127
Johnson, Una, 51
Johnson, Willard (Spud), 25
Jones, Anita Romero, 149
Jonson, Raymond, 16, 48, 57, 60,
    66, 68, 73, 146
    B. Print, 76
    Sanctuario, 73, *75*
Juárez, Roberto, 150
Jung, Carl, 25

Kandinsky, Wassily, 27
Kavin, Zena, 144
Kennedy, John F., 83
Kiley, Robert Leland, 60
Kimball, W. Wayne, Jr., 148
King, Dorothy S., 146
Kistler, Lynton, 63, 71–72, 147
Klee, Paul, 18, 51
Kline, Franz, 71
Kloss, Gene, 38–40, 57, 73;
    Sanctuary, Chimayo, The, 39
Knees and Aborigines (Sloan), 18, *22*
Kraft, Jim, 124

Kriegstein, Zara, 118
Kroll, Leon, 10
Kuniyoshi, Yasuo, 40

LaMarr, Jean, 108
Lantz, Juanita, 144
Larsson, Karl, 146
Lasansky, Mauricio, 71, 108
Lash, Kenneth, 51
Latham, Barbara, 33, 35–36, 40, 57;
    Rail, The, 37
Laughing Horse, The (magazine), 25
Layered Passages (Sprunt), 130, *131*
Leeper, John Palmer, 51
Lehrer, Leonard, 90; *Tepotzotlan*, *93*
Lieberman, William, 51
Linnell, Susan, 149
Lippincott, Janet, 90
Lobo, The (Cook), *35*
Lockwood, Ward, 27, 32, 35, 37, 73
    Taos Plaza, 27, *33*
    Taos Signs, 27, *32*
    Target, 73, *74*
Longley, Bernique, 146
Longley, William, 146
López, Félix, 136
López, Ramón, 149
Loving, Reg, 149
Lowengrund, Margaret, 72
Lowney, Bruce, 90, 111; *Gateway,
    Plate IX*, 115
Luhan, Mabel Dodge. *See* Dodge
Lumpkins, William, 146; *Untitled*,
    55–57, *56*

Madness (Fidler), *109*
Madrid, Lydia 106
Magennis, Beverly, 124
    *Partial Construction of Improbable
        Sculpture I*, *126*, 127
Mallary, Robert, 52
Man with Cane (Alvino Ortega)
    (Nordfeldt), *14*, 15
Mandelman, Beatrice, 57–59
Marin, John, 25, 27, 32, 83
Martin, Agnes, 52, 83; *On a Clear
    Day*, 84

Martínez, Eluid, 149
Masley, Alexander, 53
Masson, Andr), 64
Mattox, Charles, 75, 91
McAfee, Ila, 63–64, 145
    *Small Ranch, A ("At Evening
        Time")*, *64*
McCarthy, Joseph, 66
McCray, Dorothy, 55, 57, 60, 72; *Par
    Coeur*, 55, *Plate V*
McCulloch, Frank, 111–14, 138;
    79.5, *112*
McNeil, George, 150; *Acoma Mesa I*,
    98, *100*
Mead, Roderick, 60–66; *Summer
    Night*, *67*
Megargee, Lon, 146
Mesa Verde (Stroh), *88*
Mexican Girl (Fechin), 27, *28*
Miller, Florence, 146
Miller, George C., 63–64, 143, 144
Mirror of Life Past (Romero), *111*
Miss Ever-Ready (Yunkers), *49*
Monhoff, Frederick, 40
Monte Sol, Santa Fe, El (Rönnebeck),
    40, *43*
Montenegro, Enrique, 75; *Woman on
    a Crosswalk*, *78*
Moore, James, 103
Moran, Peter
    Burro Train, New Mexico, A, *2*, 3
    Harvest at San Juan, *3*
Moran, Thomas, 3
Morang, Alfred, 146
Morning Smokes, Taos Pueblo (Cook),
    34
Morning Sun (Baumann), 17, *Plate I*
Moskowitz, Ira, *Yei-bei-chi Masks*, *59*
Moy, Seong, 51, 145
Moyah, Courtney, 108
Moyano, Sergio, *Backstage (SFO)*,
    118, *120*
Moylan, Lloyd, 144, 146
Mozley, Loren, 44, 143
Mruk, Wladyslaw, 143
Munch, Edvard, 48

Museum of Fine Arts (Santa Fe), 80
  annual print exhibitions at, 57, 66
  controversy at, 66–69
  inaugural exhibition, 18
  "open door" policy, 10, 57
  opening of, 10

Nadler, Harry, *Grey Labyrinth*, 91, *97*
Nagatani, Patrick, *Trinitite Tempest*, 136, *137*
Namingha, Dan, 80
Naravisa Press, 118–23
Nash, Willard, *Crossbearer*, 22, *23*
National Serigraph Society, 59
Nauman, Bruce, *Earth-World*, 115, *116*
Nevelson, Louise, 83, 89
Newman, Eugene, 149
New Mexico State University, 108
Nieto, John, 149
Night Watchman, The (Hurd), 60, *62*
Nordfeldt, B. J. O., 12, 15–16, 27, 38, 139, 142
  Crucifixion, *15*
  Man with Cane (Alvino Ortega), *14*, 15
Nude in Red Kimono (Abdalla), *95*
Nusbaum, Jesse, 38

O'Hara, Frederick, 51, 55, 57, 68, 72
  Comanche Gap IV, *50*, 51
  Garden of Folly, Series II, 51, *Plate IV*
O'Keeffe, Georgia, 25, 83
Oliveira, Nathan, *Acoma Hawk V*, 98, *99*
On a Clear Day (Martin), *84*

Painter-Gravers of America, 3–4, 12
Palmore, Tom, 118
  Rare Southwestern Toucan, 124, *125*
Par Coeur (McCray), 55, *Plate V*
Parsons, Sheldon, 66
Partial Construction of Improbable Sculpture I (Magennis), 126, *127*

Peace (Bisttram), 27, *29*
Pearlstein, Philip, *Ruins at Gran Quivira*, *98*
Pearson, Ralph M., 4; *Church at Ranchos de Taos*, *8*
Pelton, Agnes, 146
Penitentes (Davey), 10, *12*
Peterdi, Gabor, 51, 71
Peterson, Robert, 130; *Shop Towel over Block*, *133*
Peterson, William, 124
Phillips, Bert, 1
Phillips, Jay, *Descent of Discord, Plate XIV*, 127
Picasso, Pablo, 22, 124, 138
Pierce, H. Towner, 146
Pieta (Tatschl), *52*
Platt, Peter, 16
Pletka, Paul, 89; *Raven*, *90*
Plums (Antreasian), 103, *104*
Popejoy, Tom L., 73
Portrait of Mrs. M. (Cassidy), 4, *6*
Pound, Ezra, 139
Prairie Print Makers, 59
Prayer for the Hunt (Shuster), *23*
Price, Kenneth, 98–100; *Untitled, Plate VIII*, 100
Prints in the Desert, 51
Profile in Blue (Ron Adams), *Plate XI*, 118
Public Works of Art Project (PWAP), 37–38
Pueblo Ceremonial Trio (Tubis), 108, *110*

Quartet EPC, I (Yates), *132*

Raffael, Joseph, 89
Rail, The (Latham), *37*
Rain (Sewards), *113*
Ranchos Valley I (Dasburg), 84, *85*
Rare Southwestern Toucan (Palmore), 124, *125*
Rauschenberg, Robert, 115
Raven (Pletka), *90*
Ravens Feeding in a Field (Schooley), *53*

Reed, Doel, *Adobe and Wild Plum*,
66, *67*
Regatta: The Start (Black), *68*
Remington, Deborah, 89
Repin, Ilya, 27
Return to A-qq #3 (Zelt), 127, *129*
Riley, Wenceslaus D., 108
Rio Grande Gorge #16 (Robert M.
Ellis), *96*
Rio Grande Graphics, 51
Rio Grande Workshop, The, 51
Ritual on the Mesa (Tait), *58*
Roberts, Dolona, 118
Roberts, Holly, 90
Rodriguez, Jos, *Sagrado Corazon*,
106, *107*
Romero, Mike, 108; *Mirror of Life
Past, 111*
Rönnebeck, Arnold, *Monte Sol, Santa
Fe, El*, 40, *43*
Roosevelt, Franklin D., 37
Roswell Museum and Art Center, 106,
108–14
Roth, Ernest, 16
Ruins at Gran Quivira (Pearlstein), *98*
Ruscha, Ed, 89
Russell, Morgan, 25
Ryan, Jeffrey, 127–30

Sagrado Corazon (Rodriguez), 106,
107
San Geronimo—Taos (Baumann),
Frontispiece, 16
Sanctuario (Jonson), 73, *75*
Sanctuary, Chimayo, The (Kloss), *39*
Sand Storm (Cassidy), 4, *7*
Sandhill South (Jaune Quick-to-See
Smith), *82, 83*
Sandia (Brach), 98, *101*
Sandia (Young), *77*
Sandoval, Bonafacio, 149
Sandzen, Birger, 4, 16, 142; *Gran
Quivira*, 8, *9*
Santa Fe New Mexican, 66
Sarkisian, Paul, 87; *Envelope (Red
Background), Plate X*, 115
Scanga, Italo, 150

Schanker, Louis, 145
Schlater, Katharine, 146
Schleeter, Howard, 60; *Glow Bugs, 61*
Scholder, Fritz, 80, 87
Indian on Galloping Horse after
Remington #2, *Plate VI*, 80
Schooley, Elmer, 53–55, 57, 60,
63, 68, 72, 143
Garden Walk, 54, 55
Ravens Feeding in a Field, 53
Scott, Sam, 89, 149; *Edge of Autumn,
91*
Seis Santeros (suite), 136
Sender, Ramón, 51
Serigraphics, 124
79.5 (McCulloch), *112*
Seward, Coy Avon, 16
Sewards, Michele Bourque, 90, 111;
Rain, 113
Shapiro, Paul, *Golem, The*, 118, *121*
Sharing Traditions (Forbis), *123*
Sharp, Joseph, 1–2, 4
Shin Hanga III (Gash), 127, *128*
Shop Towel over Block (Peterson), *133*
Shuster, Will, 18, 57, 143; *Prayer for
the Hunt, 23*
Sihvonen, Oli, 57; *Block Print IV, 60*
Simpkins, Wayne H., 148
Sloan, Dolly, 59
Sloan, Helen Farr. *See* Farr, Helen
Sloan, John, 16, 57, 59, 66, 142
Hopi Snake Dance, Walpi Mesa, 10,
11
Knees and Aborigines, 18, *22*
Small Ranch, A ("At Evening Time")
(McAfee), *64*
Smith, Jaune Quick-to-See, 80–83,
150; *Sandhill South, 82, 83*
Smith, Sam, 91
Snake and Eagle (Jimenez), *122, 123*
Snidow, Gordon, *Baby Sitter, The*, 89
*Sombras de Los Edificios Religiosos de
Nuevo México Norte, Los* (Waldrum),
124
Sommers, John, 76, 84–87, 102,
106, 114, 143
Wold (Ambience), 86, 87

Springer, Eva, 146
Sprunt, Vera Henderson, *Layered Passages*, 130, *131*
Steen, Nancy, 90, 123
Stein, Gertrude, 25
Stein, Leo, 25
Stevens, Mark, 118
Stewart, Dorothy N., 146
Strata (Clinton Adams), 76, *79*
Street Scene, Taos (Berninghaus), 4, *5*
Stringing the Bow (Hennings), 18, *19*
Stroh, Earl, 84, 87
  Mesa Verde, 88
  Symbiosis I (Stroh), *Plate VII*, 87
Succubae (Yunkers), 51, *plate II*
Summer Night (Mead), *67*
Summers, Carol, 145
Sussman, Arthur, 149
Swartz, Beth Ames, 149
Symbiosis I (Stroh), *Plate VII*, 87

Tait, Agnes, 59, 145; *Ritual on the Mesa, 58*
Takach, Dave, 100–102
Takach-Garfield Company, 102
Tamarind Institute, 76, 80–83, 87–102, 115, 127, 130–36, 139
Tamarind Lithography Workshop (Los Angeles), 72–75, 83, 114
Tamotzu, Chuzo, 145
Tanguy, Yves, 64
Taos Man (Gorman), *81*
Taos Plaza (Lockwood), 27, *33*
Taos Pueblo I (Dasburg), 25, *26*
Taos School of Art, 27
Taos Signs (Lockwood), 27, *32*
Taos Society of Artists, 4, 10, 27
Taos Tryst (Castellón), 40, *41*
Tapia, Luis, 136
Target (Lockwood), 73, *74*
Task Mask (Barrow), *Plate XV*, 130
Tatschl, John, 52, 57, 66; *Pieta, 52*
Taylor, Joshua, 36
Taylor, Prentiss, *Towards Santa Fe*, 40, *44*
Tepotzotlan (Lehrer), *93*
Thompson, Richard, 149

Towards Santa Fe (Taylor), 40, *44*
Transcendentalist Painting Group, 55
Trinitite Tempest (Nagatani), 136, *137*
Tubis, Seymour, *Pueblo Ceremonial Trio*, 108, *110*
21 Steps, 127
Tworkov, Jack, 89
Tyler, Kenneth, 115

Udall, Sharyn, 66
Ufer, Walter, 1–2, 4, 16, 142
Unified Arts, 124–27
Universal Limited Art Editions (ULAE), 72
University of New Mexico, 48, 52–53, 73, 76, 83, 90–91, 103–6
Untitled (App), 130, *135*
Untitled (Lumpkins), 55–57, *56*
Untitled (Price), *Plate VIII*, 100
Untitled (Ranchos de Taos) (Helen Blumenschein), *65*
Untitled 72–121 (Antreasian), 103, *105*
Untitled (Taos Pueblo) (Hoover), 40, *42*

Van Gogh, Vincent, 8, 48
Van Soelen, Theodore, 63–64, 145–46; *Cook, The, 63*
Van Sweringen, Norma, 146

Walch, Peter, 47
Waldrum, Harold Joe, 124
Walker, Stuart, 146
Walters, Robert, *Whorlworm*, 51, *Plate III*
Wayne, June, 72, 83, 147
Well at Quevado (Bellows drawing), 10–12, *13*
Well at Quevado (Bellows lithograph), 10–12, *13*
Wenger, John, 91
West, Harold W., 144, 146
Western Graphics Workshop and Gallery, 80, 123

Western Lithographic Company
(Wichita), 16
Western New Mexico College, 55
Westlund, Harry, 124, 148
Wet Day at the Track (Davey), 57, *58*
Weyhe, Erhard, 35
Weyhe Gallery, 35–36, 40
Whistler, James McNeill, 2–3
White, Tracy S., 148
Whorlworm (Walters), 51, *Plate III*
Wilder, Mitchell, 66, 73
Wilder, Thornton, 25
Williams, Tennesse, 25
Wilson, Thomas, 147
Witkin, Joel Peter, 124
Wold (Ambience) (Sommers), *86, 87*
Woman on a Crosswalk (Montenegro),
78

Works Progress Administration (WPA),
38–40, 71

Yates, Steve, 130; *Quartet EPC, I,
132*
Yei-bei-chi Masks (Moskowitz), *59*
Yell, Joseph E., 143
Young, Alfred, 75; *Sandia, 77*
Yunkers, Adja, 47–53, 69, 72, 139
Miss Ever-Ready, 49
Succubae, 51, *Plate II*
Yunkers, Kerstin, 48, 51
Yunkers, Nambita, 48

Zelt, Martie, *Return to A-qq #3,* 127,
129
Zigrosser, Carl, 35–36, 40, 144

PRINTMAKING IN NEW MEXICO
1880–1990

Edited by Dana Asbury
Designed by Milenda Nan Ok Lee
Typography in Bodoni
by the University of New Mexico Printing Services
Printed by Dai Nippon Printing Company
Printed in Japan